THE ART OF TRAINING YOUR DOG

THE ART OF TRAINING YOUR DOG

*How to Gently
Teach Good Behavior
Using an E-Collar*

THE MONKS OF NEW SKETE

AND

MARC GOLDBERG

PHOTOGRAPHS BY VINCENT REMINI

Countryman Press

*An Imprint of W. W. Norton & Company
Independent Publishers Since 1923*

THE ART OF TRAINING YOUR DOG is a general information resource. The instructions given are intended to be followed exactly, without skipping steps or shortening the time periods for the exercises. No two dogs are alike, however, and no recommendation will work for every dog. Product and services recommendations, if any, contained in this book are based on the authors' own experience and should not be construed as a guaranty of availability, performance, or fitness for any particular purpose. Names and potentially identifying characteristics of people and animals have been changed.

A NOTE ON SAFETY: The program described in this book is not intended to address serious canine aggression. If your dog has ever bitten someone or you believe it eventually might, you should consult an experienced dog trainer for personalized help and advice.

For information about permission to reproduce selections from this book, write to Permissions, Countryman Press, 500 Fifth Avenue, New York, NY 10110

For information about special discounts for bulk purchases, please contact W. W. Norton Special Sales at specialsales@wwnorton.com or 800-233-4830

Manufacturing by Versa Press
Book design by Lidija Tomas
Art director: Allison Chi
Production manager: Devon Zahn

Countryman Press
www.countrymanpress.com

An imprint of W. W. Norton & Company, Inc.
500 Fifth Avenue, New York, NY 10110
www.wwnorton.com

Library of Congress Cataloging-in-Publication Data

Names: Goldberg, Marc (Dog trainer), author. | Remini, Vincent, photographer.
Title: The art of training your dog : how to gently teach good behavior using an e-collar / The Monks of New Skete and Marc Goldberg ; photographs by Vincent Remini.
Description: New York, NY : The Countryman Press, [2020] | Includes index.
Identifiers: LCCN 2020031426 | ISBN 9781682685020 (hardcover) | ISBN 9781682685037 (epub)
Subjects: LCSH: Dogs—Training. | Dog collars—Technological innovations.
Classification: LCC SF431 .G65 2020 | DDC 636.7/0835—dc23
LC record available at https://lccn.loc.gov/2020031426

ISBN 978-1-68268-761-1 pbk.

10 9 8 7 6 5 4 3 2 1

To my brothers and sisters of New Skete. Over the years, you have supported me in my work with dogs. Your constant encouragement has always inspired me to be a better person, monk, and trainer.

—Brother Christopher

For my father, Barney Goldberg, who gave me his profound love of dogs. For my mother, Neshama Siner, who helped me live my dream. And for my sister, Meredith, who preferred cats but learned to love a dog.

—Marc Goldberg

CONTENTS

INTRODUCTION

"From a spiritual perspective, there is no limit to the change, growth, and maturity that a human being can undergo; the wonder is that, in its own way, the same is true of the dog. Dogs can always grow in learning and responsiveness, in attentiveness and bonding, significantly broadening the parameters of what most of us think is possible from a relationship."

—The Monks of New Skete, *Bless the Dogs*

Dogs are loving and intuitive beings. They possess far greater complexity than a simple collection of instincts. They have emotions and individual preferences. Because dogs don't always know what's best and safest for them in the human world, we have to teach them. To do that, first we must understand them.

Like all other professions, dog training is a dynamic field. Among the many theories of training, some directly contradict others. Perhaps there's no right or wrong way, but training today looks different from 100, 50, or even 25 years ago. Certainly, trainers themselves change as they learn. The more time you put into a vocation or activity, the more skills you attain.

During the training process, the transformation that takes place in dogs and their owners continues to thrill and awe us as longtime professional trainers. Dogs' behaviors moving from chaotic and random to alert and attentive proves rewarding on many levels. It can mean security and safety as well as joy and pleasure. Well-behaved dogs have a positive effect on the health and well-being of their owners. Similar results are clear for the dogs, too. When their vital needs are met and they fit in their owners' lives, well-trained dogs wear their confidence all over their bodies. It's inspiring to watch the potential in the human-dog relationship unlock. A fulfilling process, training stretches the possibilities inherent in that relationship.

Most dog owners begin training with the goal of getting their dogs to *stop naughty behaviors*, rather than starting with the positive goal of what they want their dogs to *do instead*. That's why we talk about how to stop bad behavior and also explore the reasons that dogs tend to misbehave in the first place. Once we understood those reasons ourselves, our training became easier, more elegant, and more fun for the dogs and for us.

As with so many trainers, our love of dogs began in childhood. What a wonderful advantage, during those formative years, to have dogs in our homes. Dogs teach so many critical lessons to children, including how to recognize the needs of others and to understand that sometimes those needs must come first.

Our collaboration reflects many cumulative years of training and living with dogs, and our work has evolved over time. We cut our teeth on traditional methods, always with a view to helping dogs and their owners live more harmoniously with one another. Over the decades, we have improved and refined our methods into a modern and compassionate approach that allows people and their dogs to live together happily and with greater understanding. Our daily experience leads the way. For us, obedience training represents a spiritual discipline as much as an artful use of technique. Training dogs means guiding them to understand obedience commands and holding them accountable to obey them. This balanced approach combines plenty of motivational praise and positive reinforcement with appropriate corrections when necessary. Our training always serves the relationship and proves reliable in everyday life.

The more we work with dogs, the more they teach us, both about their nature and our own. As we figured out what worked and what didn't, we saw that listening to what dogs need and want would become a lifelong, ever-changing process. Precisely for this reason, we always seek new ways to make our training gentler and more effective. In recent years, we have witnessed the introduction of new tools into the process, everything from clickers to head halters.

When Marc Goldberg, a nationally renowned trainer, first came across the modern electronic collar (e-collar) and began to develop his method, he saw it not as just a do-this-do-that training method, but rather as a holistic approach to living with a dog that brings out the best in human and canine alike, without using heavy compulsion. His approach blended seamlessly with the philosophy that the monks have advocated for years and provided the basis for working together as friends and colleagues. About 15 years ago, the Monks of New Skete incorporated the e-collar into their training, using methods developed by Marc. This transformational tool has become an integral part of daily training activities for Brother Christopher and Marc. The reason is simple yet surprising: With an enlightened program of e-collar training, dogs learn faster, with more enjoyment and far less stress. Our method allows for gentle training of a dog to previously unrealized levels of freedom. What so many owners dream about—drama-free walks around the neighborhood or off-leash reliability in nature— becomes a possibility with proper e-collar training. It makes for happier dogs, which can exercise and enjoy their place in our world more safely.

We have experienced firsthand the opportunities and benefits that our method creates. This approach doesn't come from textbooks used in veterinary schools, though we believe it aligns with the best that we know of canine behavior. Given our enthusiastic convictions, it makes sense to share how we became involved with it, what we describe as a "conversion," though not one that took place in any church or synagogue. It occurred in the context of working with dogs directly and helping them live better lives. We will describe these moments in the first two chapters.

When most people think of dog training, they tend to see it as the

Good e-collar training is fun for both the dog and the trainer

process of getting dogs to do what they inherently *don't* want to do. Emphasis too often falls on one-dimensional negatives: what they want the dogs to stop doing and the force they're willing to use to achieve that goal. Consequently, many owners consider corrective training a necessary evil, something to make it possible to live with their dogs, but about which they feel uneasy or guilty.

On the other hand, a vast majority of our training clients have tried what's commonly misnamed "all-positive training" before coming to us. This form of training relies heavily on food to motivate compliance but quickly falls apart for dogs who don't care about treats or who aren't hungry. Worse yet, it instantly breaks down for all dogs when they become highly distracted. All too often, the dogs won't keep their noses out of the trash can, let alone behave calmly at the kids' soccer games.

Isolation, frequent scolding, or both often result. Mind you, we're not saying that the occasional leash correction is always bad, nor are we saying that food rewards are never useful. But training methods that rely exclusively on either method likely exert excessive physical or psychological force on the dog. Neither approach will produce the results that a conscientious dog owner truly wants.

An e-collar, when used with understanding by an educated owner or trainer, plays a vital role in the humane training of a dog. We have experienced firsthand how this tool can transform the human-dog relationship. It's revolutionary and evolutionary. It moves training to new levels of possibility. The results have astonished and gratified many dog owners who followed the method and shared their testimonies with us.

Permit us to share a success story. Over the course of 6 weeks, a gentleman named Shane, who belonged to our Facebook group (about which you will find more below), asked questions and shared videos of his progress, keeping the group informed about his training journey. Weller, his dog, went from a wild boy to a well-behaved companion who eventually became trustworthy during off-leash hikes, which both owner and dog loved. Nearly a year later, man and dog made the news when, dressed in a doggy tuxedo, Weller served as "best man" at Shane's wedding.

Training must take place with compassion, intelligence, and insight, with the benefit of a method clearly and easily understood by both owner and dog. You may wonder whether you can do the training program in this book without an e-collar, and the answer is yes. Even if you don't use an e-collar, you will benefit from working through the lessons. Your training likely won't advance to full off-leash control as easily as if you don't use one according to our program. Still, there's no such thing as bad improvement. You'll make progress either way.

Every dog matures at a slightly different rate, but we find that most dogs are ready for our method around the age of 5 months. A puppy under 1 year of age tends to have a shorter attention span. Most of our lessons are fairly brief, but if you sense your puppy tiring in the middle of a lesson, end it early and on a good note. You always can do another short session after your dog rests. As long as you have a healthy pet, no upper age limit applies. Indeed, we have trained many older dogs. You also may wonder about size. We'll introduce you to e-collars rated for dogs as small as 5 pounds.

Still, a word of caution: The e-collar isn't a magic wand. Like any tool, if used crudely or in an unenlightened way, it can have harmful effects. Some who have never observed its proper use deplore it. We go into detail about this controversy in Chapter 3, responding to those who criticize the use of e-collars with dogs. Our purpose here is much broader than a simple defense of e-collars, however. We passionately want to help you and other owners understand how to use this tool gracefully and in an enlightened manner that serves the human-dog relationship and allows you to trust how your dog will respond in a variety of situations.

In this book, by integrating the best in modern technology with all that we have learned about dog behavior since we wrote *How to Be Your Dog's Best Friend* in 1978, we build on dogs' pack instincts to shape their behavior, using painless, low-level electronic signals for attention, matched with clear body language to indicate what we want, followed quickly by rewards to teach the dogs in a positive manner. As learning increases, we integrate the training into everyday life to create reliably good behavior that owners can trust. The result is a willing, happy partner in the human-dog relationship and in the training process itself. We aim to maximize the freedom that owner and dog can experience together, allowing the dog to be managed safely and reliably even in off-leash situations.

You can find many opinions about e-collars on the internet and in professional circles. These range from entirely negative to entirely positive. The truth lies between the extremes. If used well, with compassion and planning, the e-collar offers a positive opportunity to shape a dog's behavior and, by extension, the

Dogs are happiest when they can accompany their owners

relationship between owner and dog. If used without preparation and punitively, the training will fail to achieve its potential. The effects of training, good or bad, are always visible on the dog and in the relationship with the owner. A dog trained by a bullying owner won't appear at ease. One trained by an overly permissive owner won't respond reliably to commands. The ultimate truth resides in that relationship. Good training makes for a good relationship.

That said, we know how difficult it can be for owners to find reliable information, let alone a step-by-step method that guides them safely through all areas of dog training and problem behaviors. That's what motivated us to present our approach in book form. It has been enormously gratifying to receive so much positive feedback from dog lovers who have followed the method with much success.

That accomplishment motivated us to refine our understanding of how to use this remarkable tool artfully and skillfully with our dogs, and the opportunity of this paperback edition similarly excites us. We have an occasion to make the book even better. Since the book's initial publication, we formed a Facebook group, The Art of

Training Your Dog with an Ecollar, where thousands of members regularly share questions and observations about the method. Along with dozens of fellow trainers, we answer questions, share videos of the lessons, and help our readers train their dogs in a kindly, effective manner. All readers of this book are welcome to join the group, which provides an additional resource to help you achieve your dreams for your dog.

Using social media to complement the instructions in this book takes dog training further into the 21st century, creating a community of dog owners who benefit from one another's insights and encouragement. It has been fascinating to see how our readers are connecting better with their dogs. They become better owners and, in some ways, better people. Participating in our system functions as a sort of sacred practice in which the difference between everyday contact and purposeful communication becomes the keystone of training success.

We have multiple goals for this new edition. First and most importantly, we want to help you achieve a better and more profound relationship with your dog. "A tired dog is a good dog," the old saw goes, but one of our clients said to us: "A trained dog is a happier dog." We firmly believe that because we see it every day in our work with our own dogs and clients' dogs. A trained dog is freed from conflict, nagging, scolding, and, where appropriate, even the leash. Second, we want to give you our professional perspective on the controversy surrounding e-collars to help you make up your own mind. Third, we explain which collars and features we like best and why. In the second half of the book, which includes new information, we guide you, step by step, through how we train dogs to off-leash reliability so you can recreate our results safely and economically with your own dog. We also will give you our best advice to help you to stop your dog from behaving in an unsafe or destructive manner.

We'll teach you the "how to" of dog training in a series of logical steps, but we'll start by explaining the nature of the human-canine relationship and how we came to understand it. Once you comprehend what your dog needs and wants, the training lessons and their goals make better sense and you'll be well positioned to help your dog learn them. In this paperback edition, we also provide additional lesson notes in the form of a Frequently Asked Questions section (page 274) that arises from questions that clients and readers often ask us.

WELCOME TO 21ST-CENTURY DOG TRAINING

We are on the brink of a revolution in dog training. The method we present in this book offers your dog freedom from conflict and freedom of movement. It also offers you freedom from worry; you can help make your dog safer and happier. Your own transformation is coming. We assure you that all of this can be done gently and by most people over the course of 6 weeks. Follow the program we will give you; do not be tempted to skip steps even when your dog is doing well, and we believe you'll be shaking your head in amazement. We know this because, for the first few years, we did the same.

Brother Christopher
and a 6-week-old
New Skete German
shepherd puppy

CHAPTER 1

The Monks of New Skete

How is it that a monk is coauthoring a book on e-collar training for dogs? Probably the same way the Monks of New Skete ended up with a television show on Animal Planet and the way we happened to sell over a million dog books, becoming *New York Times* best-selling authors along the way. It is the culmination of a fascinating and unexpected journey. However, to provide a fuller understanding of this journey, I have to go back into the history of the monastic community that I am a part of: New Skete monastery. The Monks of New Skete story began in 1966, when a group of Franciscan brothers founded the community. They wanted to live a more authentically Orthodox monastic life than was possible in the community they came from. They were young, idealistic, and willing to work energetically for the vision they sought. After a few temporary residences that allowed them to hammer out the principles they would live by, the monks finally settled on Two-Top Mountain outside the small village of Cambridge, New York, building the monastery themselves.

To support ourselves during those difficult first years of our existence, the monks operated a farm complete with meat and dairy cattle, goats, chickens, pheasants, pigs, and sheep. From the very start, our life was deeply connected with the land and with nature. We wanted to live in harmony not only with the ideals of St Francis of Assisi but also with the precepts of Christian monasticism more broadly. Monks have always had an intense reverence for nature and animals because both reveal something important about the mystery of God.

From the very start, the brothers lived with a pet German shepherd named Kyr, who came with us from our former monastery. Kyr was a stabilizing influence during those challenging first years, because he wouldn't let things get too serious. He loved to play and showed a generosity of heart that all the brothers responded to. Further, working with farm animals sensitized them to the emotional lives of animals and provided an ideal introduction to animal psychology and behavior. While we did not realize it at the time, this was the root from which we evolved into professional breeders and trainers of dogs.

When it became clear in the late '60s that our farm could not economically sustain the community, a series of notable events shepherded us into the world of dogs and then into the public eye. The first was tragic: Kyr died when the monks were in the process of building their monastery on Two-Top Mountain. We felt the loss so deeply that the community decided it was imperative to replace him. We did, obtaining two female German shepherds from a very fine breeder in nearby Massachusetts who offhandedly suggested we consider breeding them. While this was not the reason we got the dogs, it occurred to the brothers that this idea might possibly add a new and happier dimension to the farm. So, without any advance planning, these two females, Bekky and Jesse, came to serve as the foundation for what was to become the highly regarded Monks of New Skete breeding program. More importantly, they also brought back a quality of joy to the community that had been missing since Kyr's death.

Brother Thomas spearheaded our entry into living with and breeding dogs. He was one of the founding monks and was a natural dog person with a keen interest in breeding and training dogs. Bekky and Jesse gave him the opportunity to pursue both activities. He translated this passion into our expanding involvement with "everything dog" and used his natural gift for dealing with them to guide our involvement in both breeding and training. His passion was contagious, and he started to mentor the other monks in how to train and care for dogs. Brother Thomas emphasized "listening" to the dog, reading her body language, and discerning from that her real needs rather than crassly imposing our own demands on the dog. The dog needed to be respected as a dog. His approach was a perfect blend of intuition and leadership that arose naturally out of the spiritual atmosphere of the monastery. The result was a unique approach that benefited both dogs and monks alike. While Bekky and Jesse thrived (as well as a growing number of resident dogs), caring

The Monks of New Skete live closely with their dogs, who have learned to be a well-behaved pack

for them demanded of each brother a sense of responsibility and commitment, responding to the needs of another creature regardless of how one felt. That helped each of us mature and deepened the relationship each monk had with the dogs.

Seeing the positive effect this was having on the community confirmed our decision to have each monk care for one or two dogs and gave us the possibility of starting a viable breeding program. This meant we needed to train our dogs to live as a well-behaved pack to maintain the quiet and order so necessary for a monastery. As we bred and acquired more dogs, our pack expanded. We were surprised by how much magic they brought to our monastic lives. Visitors began to comment that they wished their dogs would behave as well as they saw ours behaving. That planted a seed, so to meet the need we inaugurated a training program that reflected our developing approach. Before long we were training other people's dogs in a 3-week

Breeding and training dogs has long been part of the New Skete community's mission

boarding program. This was good for the dogs and their owners, but also for the monks. Not only were the dogs helping us survive economically, they were also having a profound effect on our spiritual lives; they were helping us become better monks.

As the years passed, our breeding and training programs grew. Newspapers and magazines began to write about this community of monks who lived with well-behaved German shepherds that accompanied them throughout the day, who bred dogs carefully and also trained dogs for customers. Through serious study as well as living closely with our dogs, we sought to deepen the relationship between people and dogs. Tragically, in 1973, Brother Thomas died in a car accident. Because the Monks of New Skete are a community, other brothers stepped up to continue what they had learned from him. Each contributed his own insights and gifts. By this time the breeding and training programs were stable. Our reputation grew largely through word of mouth and the occasional article.

But our quiet life of obscurity was soon to change. In the mid-'70s a man brought his dog for training at the monastery. He traveled to the monastery from New York City. This man was struck by the positive changes in his dog and what he learned from the monks.

"This is amazing. You should write a book!" he exclaimed.

"What do we know about writing books?" we answered.

"We're simple dog-training monks."

In a twist of fate, it turned out that the man was an editor at a major publishing company. He suggested we write a book about our approach and offered to explain the process. *How to Be Your Dog's Best Friend,* still selling and still in hardcover, has sold over half a million copies. It quickly struck a chord with the public, articulating what dog lovers craved: not a religious but a spiritual dimension to their relationship. At the same time the book provided clear guidance on teaching obedience exercises and integrating them into daily life. Famously, the book shows photographs of our dogs calmly resting with us in recreation, lying down at meals, walking in the woods, even sleeping with us in our bedrooms. No one has been more surprised than us that the book has been in continuous publication since 1978.

As for myself, I came to New Skete in 1981. I never thought I would be a dog trainer. While I grew up with dogs and loved them, they were house pets who were never formally trained. OK, so that's not the whole story. To be honest, we loved them, but my family unfailingly spoiled them. All of them. Since most were small dogs, we could get away with this as long as they were housetrained. Only one was a larger dog, a German shepherd named Colonel who was given to us by a friend, but after several months we had to place him with a local farmer because he was too difficult for us to handle. Translated, that means he put the fear of God into the neighborhood, and my parents realized disaster was imminent if we didn't place him quickly. But soon after, we adopted Queenie, a 6-pound toy Manchester terrier my dad got from the Humane Society. I was an only child, and Queenie provided important companionship for me. She was feisty enough to hold her own in the face of my good-natured teasing. She slept in my room at night and would unfailingly get me up in the morning to let her out before school. I shared feeding responsibilities with my mother, and while Queenie wasn't exactly the proverbial "neighborhood dog" who shadowed me at baseball games and during rounds of hide-and-go-seek, she was an important part of my early childhood and high school years. She continued to live with my parents until she was 20, well after I had left home and graduated from college.

People who know New Skete often assume that the reason I came here was because the monastery bred German shepherds and trained dogs of all breeds. Actually, that had nothing to do with my decision. When I graduated from college, I was deeply drawn to spiritual life. Monasticism seemed to provide the opportunity to do this in a full-time, intentional way. I joined New Skete because it offered a perfect blend of monastic spirituality and communal living. "Monasticism with a human face" is how our small community of 12 monks described itself. While I knew that the community was known for its work with dogs—and I found it attractive to live with a dozen or so German shepherds—the real reason I came was that I wanted to be a monk. New Skete felt like a place where I could do that and be happy.

When you say the word *monk*, most people have the image of a person who prays a lot. And we do. But that's not all we do. In fact, monasticism has as its goal a balanced life of prayer, work, and communal living, and we do this in a structured way, striving to live prayerfully in each of the areas of our life. Since monasteries are self-supporting, work is a central part of each day. Monasteries have long been known for the quality products they produce: jams and preserves, cheeses, incense, liturgical vestments, gourmet candies, cookies, bonsai trees, and even cheesecakes. While at one time we produced fresh sausage, smoked meats, and cheeses, in recent years we have focused entirely on our dog programs, and that is what New Skete is most known for. So, understandably, when I first joined the Monks of New Skete, I worked in a variety of areas, getting a basic idea of each of them. As for the dogs, I helped Brother Job, who was the head trainer at that time. I assisted him once or twice a week, serving as a distraction while he tested clients' dogs before they went home. During that first year I got a basic sense of what the training program involved and how to manage one of our own German shepherds who had been assigned to me. I also imbibed the spirit of how dogs were integrated into the community and connected with them in much the same way the monks did in the early years.

I served as Brother Job's part-time dog training assistant for a year. And then, as fate would have it, he abruptly left the monastery. He left behind a kennel filled with dogs. I was the only brother who had the time and freedom to take Job's place. When the abbot asked me to step in as head dog trainer, I said I'd give it a try but asked if we could we lower the price for our clients until I was certain I could produce the results our customers deserved. "No way," the abbot said. "The price stays the same." That meant I had to get up to speed quickly.

My journey to become a good dog trainer was a baptism of fire, but it propelled me to become a passionate student of canines. What I lacked in experience I made up for in effort. For the next 12 months, I ate, slept, and studied with dogs on my mind. I relied on *How to Be Your Dog's Best Friend* as if it were a bible, and I devoured all the other dog books in our extensive library. My brother monks indulged my endless questions. It took me three times longer to train a dog than a normal trainer. But when I saw the transformation taking place in the dogs I was training and started getting positive feedback from their owners, I fell in love with the work and discovered an essential part of my calling.

For the next 25 years I used the monastery as a laboratory for training, working with all manner of breeds and progressively refining my skills as a trainer. I also wrote several books with the monks, including *The Art of Raising a Puppy*. I helped produce a video series on training as well as the TV show that aired on Animal Planet. As I look back, I realize the training I specialized in during this time was old school, a personalized version of what I originally learned. Our priority was then—and remains now—dog training as a bridge that builds a wholesome relationship, spanning the gap between human and dog. Since we had already written two very popular training books from our monastic perspective, I didn't imagine there could be anything more for me to write about basic training that wouldn't be redundant. This left me free to explore a subject I was endlessly fascinated with: the deeper spiritual connection between humans and dogs. Living in a contemplative monastery naturally sensitizes one to this, so I put down my own observations with the hope that they might resonate with and inspire dog owners of all kinds. I wrote two meditation books that combined beautiful photographs with short reflections to celebrate how dogs touch us in our spiritual depths, regardless of religious affiliation or lack thereof. It was creative work that blended my love for dogs with my love for writing and was deeply fulfilling.

Throughout these years, I still trained dogs every day, successfully using the methods we had written about in our earlier books. E-collars did not appear on my radar. Yes, I knew them to be tools to solve extreme problems, ones that threatened a dog's life, such as killing livestock. In that context I believed they could have value, but I didn't see their use in the obedience training I had been doing for 25 years. Put very simply, I figured that if I had to shock a dog to get him to obey, I was a pretty deficient trainer. All that changed in 2006, when I had a conversation with Wendy Volhard, author and internationally respected dog trainer. We were both at a conference and got to talking about the world of dogs.

She asked me pointedly what I thought about e-collars. I gave her my standard response as above, and she looked at me very seriously. "You know," she said, "I had exactly the same attitude until recently. Then I hosted Marc Goldberg for several days at my home. He volunteered to show me and some of my colleagues how he used the e-collar in working with dogs, both for ordinary training and for dealing with problems. I'll be honest: at first, I was skeptical. But I have to say that during those days I saw him use the e-collar in such a graceful, elegant way. It was enlightening to say the least, and I just didn't have him work with easy dogs, either. I had lined up a number of challenging dogs, and he worked with those kindly and extremely well. Here's what I'd advise you do: take a seminar from him and see for yourself. Given your own work with dogs, I think you owe it to yourself to go into it with an open mind. So much has changed in the technology."

So I did. I arranged to attend a seminar Marc was conducting with Martin Deeley in Florida. What I witnessed at the seminar was nothing short of astonishing: a way to dramatically improve dog training in a manner absolutely consonant with the philosophical principles the Monks of New Skete stood for. I saw two seasoned professionals share what they had discovered not just about e-collars but also about how to use them artfully and how that could blend seamlessly with my own experience as a trainer. Their methods were gentle and quite subtle. Over the course of that weeklong seminar I saw previously untrained dogs respond happily and with quick understanding to the training they were being given. At the end of the week, I faced a challenge: I now knew that using this method could be an even more humane

The Transfiguration Church was designed and built by the Monks in the 1970s

and effective approach than the way I had been training for many years, so did I have a moral and spiritual responsibility to integrate it into the program I was running? I believed I did, yet I knew such a decision would be controversial. I decided to trust my experience as well as my own knowledge and love of dogs. It's a decision I've never regretted.

The welcome porch has been made possible
by a generous gift from:

Marc Goldberg

In honor of the dogs who taught him

CHAPTER 2

Marc's Practical Approach

I began training dogs when I was 11 years old. In 1969 I was given a Sheltie pup for my birthday. I named him Gus. When he was 5 months old, he ran into the street and was hit by a car. After he was patched up, my mother enrolled us in dog school. We won first prize in the graduation competition and Gus lived to nearly 18 years of age. Back then, dog training could be a little harsh compared with good technique today. Mind you, one might be able to say the same thing about child rearing. But I was a child myself, teaching a sensitive young dog, and early on I found that I didn't need to yank him quite as hard as some of the other students with bigger and more rambunctious dogs. Plus, Gus was my best friend, and I wanted him to like me.

Once the class ended, I was hooked on the idea of having a dog who listened to me. The new level our relationship was reaching meant that not only was Gus safer but he could go everywhere with me. For years, no one in any corner of Broomall, Pennsylvania, saw me without Gus, usually in the company of my close friend Arthur.

Arthur, Gus, and I, humans not even teenagers yet, boldly marched into every store within walking distance. Heel means a dog walks with his head always staying even with your left leg, even when you turn or change pace. The dog has to truly understand what is being asked of him and will have to make many adjustments of his position and speed to maintain the heel and perform it correctly. Critically, he'll have to ignore any and all distractions in the environment to focus on his handler and the job at hand. It's actually quite beautiful to see a dog and owner in complete harmony. At its best, heeling can make you feel like you're performing a sort of

A dog who is well behaved on leash can accompany you almost anywhere

ballet with your dog. It's a mental connection as well as a physical one. Gus heeled into Woolworth's, the bookstore, the gift shop, and even the grocery store. Because he was so quiet and well behaved, no employee ever thought to say anything. Gus had mastered this skill completely. Yet I was concerned when I first taught it to him because I was shown how to give him a series of nagging yanks, creating something he would want to avoid while he learned to earn praise by staying in the heel position. It bothered me that this beautiful exercise was introduced in a negative manner. Because I was a child and my dog was sensitive, I know I moderated the corrections to be fairly light, so I don't look back with regret. But I was always looking for ways to make training softer and gentler. I first discovered my passion for training dogs with Gus, and that has continued throughout my life.

After we finished obedience school, I found no additional classes for me to take with Gus. However, I was quite a reader. I devoured every book involving dogs in the Paxon Hollow Junior High School library, which caught the librarian's attention.

> *"You have read every dog book we have,"* Mrs. Chesterfield said.
> *"Do you want to be a veterinarian?"*
> *"No,"* I answered, *"I'm training my dog, and I want to learn everything I can about dog behavior."*
> Her eyes lit up. *"You're training dogs? Can you come train my dogs?"* she immediately asked.
> *"I can try,"* I said, *"but so far I have only trained my own."*

Mrs. Chesterfield said she would call my mother for permission. My mother apparently gave it, because Mrs. Chesterfield drove me to her home that afternoon and introduced me to two wild, jumping, leg-scratching black and tan standard dachshunds. I knew what breed they were because of my reading, though I had never seen dachshunds in person before. I told Mrs. Chesterfield to look out the window while I took them into the front yard to work with them.

I used the techniques I had learned in dog school. I don't know who was more surprised that they quickly began to calm down and pay attention: the dogs, Mrs. Chesterfield, or me. Later that afternoon when she dropped me at my house, Mrs. Chesterfield gave me a $5 bill! That was amazing because my weekly allowance was only $2, and I had to mow the grass or shovel the snow and take out the garbage for that. Thus were my humble beginnings as a professional dog trainer.

As I grew up I took private clients more regularly. I even taught dog training classes for the night school when I enrolled in college at Franklin & Marshall. I'm sure it was the first dog class, and maybe the last, ever offered by the college. By and large I did what my early teachers taught me, and it usually worked. But I often felt mildly worried when I had to correct a dog in a physical way. Naturally we never hit our dogs or abused them, but teaching a dog a new skill could call for strategic yanks or "pops" on the leash, which was connected to a metal slip collar given the unfortunate name of a "choke chain."

In the late '70s a book came out which was to have a huge impact on me and the way I would come to think about dogs and training. *How to Be Your Dog's Best Friend,* by the Monks of New Skete, presented not only a training technique but also a philosophy that was, at the time, truly revolutionary. Their philosophy was that dog training consisted of much more than making a dog obey a series of commands. Instead, training was meant to build and serve the relationship between dog and owner. Training, rather than turning dogs into obedient robots, could free the dog's mind, body, and spirit to flourish in the company of his best friend so both could enjoy a fuller life with one another. I became fascinated by this community of monks who famously bred German shepherds and trained them for a higher purpose: so that the dogs could share life with them and accompany them from bedroom to dining hall to long walks in the monastery's woods. Even the photographs from that book inspired me to think about how I could do more, not only for my own dogs but for others who were struggling with their dogs. Little did I know then that one day I would not only become personally acquainted with the Monks of New Skete, but I would form close friendships and write books with them.

Fast-forward many years and I became an adult with decades of dog training experience under my belt. Although I went into publishing and sales, I often took private dog training clients and taught classes as well. My method of training dogs had changed little over the years, mostly because what I was doing continued to work, ever since Gus and that pair of dachshunds.

In the mid-'90s I adopted a retired racing greyhound. Bobbi was a lovely and willing dog. She, like Gus, was very sensitive. But after adopting her from the racetrack, I realized she urgently needed to learn to come when called and not to bolt out open doors. You can't chase a greyhound. They run almost 40 miles per hour. After a couple of heart-stopping instances where Bobbi charged out the door and ran blazing laps around the house, I enrolled in a local class where I could focus on being the student rather than the teacher.

That's where I met and became good friends with trainer Mary Mazzeri. Decades earlier, Mary personally studied under famous trainer and author William Koehler. Bill's dog training books were huge sellers. His philosophy was that a dog chooses his own actions based on his learning experiences. He broke every exercise down into many steps, which he taught the dog one at a time to make the process easier for the dog. And he influenced the dog's desire to comply through reward or correction, depending on a dog's decision. It sounded rather technical, but Mary brought the Koehler method to life for me in a way the books never really had. Although I was skeptical at first, Mary challenged me to compare the method with what I had been doing for years. Much to my chagrin, I found that the highly sequential Koehler method seemed to work more quickly and reliably than all those nagging leash yanks I mentioned earlier.

Although I liked this new (to me) method and committed to learning it thoroughly, I still sought ways to soften it, so I went as light with the discipline as I could while still getting reliable results. Bobbi learned to stop bolting out doors and to come when called. Eventually I could call her off a squirrel simply by speaking her name. We had the basics down fairly well in a matter of only 10 weeks, but that squirrel thing took nearly a year of daily practice to become foolproof.

In those days, client dogs rarely got to the point where Bobbi did: reliable around rabbits and squirrels even when off leash. For most dogs and their owners, there just weren't months and months to invest in off-leash training, testing, and proofing. The reality is that, using traditional methods, it takes an immense amount of time to teach off-leash-reliable behavior because you have to start with a leash to teach it and then very gradually wean the dog off it. But the method works if you have the patience and skill to persevere with it.

So even though I was benefiting from a more structured approach to dog training, one which I softened as best I could to suit the temperament of each dog, I was still looking for more. What I really wanted was a dog training method that was gentler, that the dog enjoyed, and most important, that produced a dog that could more quickly be liberated from the leash. I was really ripe for a change, but I was not prepared for the change that Mary suggested. Somewhere around 1999 she thought we should visit a dog trainer who was using a new generation of e-collars.

I was in for a surprise. While what I witnessed wasn't entirely to my liking, what I saw planted a seed that got me thinking. I saw dogs quickly learning commands, ones that I knew took me much longer to teach. But it troubled me I did not see happy dogs with the joyful interaction between trainer and dog that I valued so highly. And I wondered why. Why couldn't the rapid learning that I was observing be combined with praise and encouraging body language? In short, why couldn't this device be used in a manner that got the results I wanted while enhancing the depth of the relationship trainer and dog shared? I suspected it could. Watching the demonstration excited the trainer in me, and I left that seminar with a deep curiosity about whether these newer e-collars could be used better and more artfully than what I had been shown.

I had several challenges to solve if I was going to use this new technology to help me get better behavior and, critically, a better relationship with dogs. What would I want to use the collar for? It seemed most logical to use it as a correction device. That's how it had always been used. But I didn't like that idea. Besides, I had seen a trainer use it as a teaching tool, though not in a way that maximized its potential. At least that's what I strongly suspected. So teaching with the e-collar quickly became my goal. But how to use it kindly? Clearly I was going to have to modify what I had observed before, but could I combine it with what I already knew about working with dogs?

Technology would help. The equipment had evolved dramatically in the 25 or 30 years since I first held an e-collar in my hands. Later in this book, we'll talk a lot more about current equipment. For the moment, suffice it to say that there had been tremendous evolution and advancements in the technology that continue to this day. But the methodology just wasn't there to use it wisely. And that's where the work would have to go: to develop a way of applying what had previously been used unkindly in a new and radically better way. Yes, I wanted to solve behavior problems and teach commands. But most of all, what brought Brother Christopher and me together was a shared sense that as a team we could refine and blend relationship-oriented dog training with artful e-collar education. We had a joint dream of helping people realize what is possible in a relationship with a dog. By using the e-collar as an educational tool, we help a dog quickly and gently develop the muscle memory needed to respond to his owner in a way that will make the dog safer, allowing him to spend more time in the company of his family. And we know that will please both parties.

From Good Dog to Great Dog

To realize the dream you have for your dog and fully benefit from the method we present here, it is important to understand some background about the human/dog relationship. Few people buy or rescue a dog so they have a pet to boss around or even to train. Nor do they usually bring a dog into the home to perform any specific job. In most of the cases we see, people acquire a dog to fulfill an emotional need: love and companionship. Lest anyone tell you this is a bad thing, let's put this up front: One of the highest callings a dog can have is as best friend to a child, a buddy to an adult, or a companion to the elderly. Ideally, dogs bring out the best in people as they help us focus on the needs of another being, get our eyes off our mobile screens, and reconnect us to nature. Our health, emotional state, and even our humanness owe a debt of gratitude to the canine species over the millennia and, in these isolating times, now more than ever.

But if we're not mindful of how we repay the debt, we humans may accidentally fall into a pattern which suits us more than the dog. Whether you realize it or not, you are training your dog from the moment you first meet her. If you worry you wouldn't like to be locked in a crate occasionally, you may be very reluctant to crate train your puppy or rescue dog. The unintended consequence is that she

Good training brings out the best in the relationship

learns she may roam freely through the house before she is ready for that, allowing her to chew or potty on anything, and if you have an objection you'll state it loudly and inconsistently. What your dog learns in these cases is that she can do whatever she wants with whatever she can reach . . . until you are upset. A bonus lesson is, although she is bonded to you, you're an occasionally loud and inconsistent creature. She'll love you for sure because that's what dogs do for members of their pack, but she'll also ignore you as needed, much like background noise.

In fact, you likely *were* occasionally locked in a crate when you were very young and able to easily harm yourself by chewing a wire or swallowing small objects. Chances are your parents put you safely in a crib or playpen when you were very young. They did this to protect you until you were old enough and well behaved enough to safely enjoy more liberty.

The spirit of a dog flourishes when he understands what is expected of him

Too many people smother their dogs with affection, not in addition to education but in place of it. Don't misunderstand us here. We love our dogs and we certainly expect you to do the same. But our first role to our dogs, like our children, isn't "buddy." It's to protect and educate them so they may thrive and become productive, living up to their full potential. It is from a combination of discipline—which we define as meaningful guidance—and education tempered with love that the deepest levels of relationship spring. Parents have to accept the responsibility that they know what is in the best interests of their children, and the same goes for us with our dogs.

That means parenting isn't always fun. If only playing with our children and dogs were enough! Anyone who has ever insisted that a 2-year-old not pull a lamp down by the cord, who has persuaded a 6-year-old to eat her vegetables, a 10-year-old to do her homework, or a 16-year-old to remember his curfew has experienced the responsible side of parenting. Yet it is critical that parents teach their children to be safe and productive members of society who may grow, thrive, and prosper. It is only later, in adulthood, when children can look back on the parents who raised them and fully understand the value of that parenting.

Why, then, is it such a struggle for so many of us to do it for our dogs?

We believe many people adopt or purchase dogs today with the mistaken belief that their dogs won't like them if they crate them even for appropriate lengths of time in a good-sized enclosure. Similarly, they fear the dog will not bond to them if they enforce rules. In short, many people raise their dogs not so much as owners but more like friends who can enjoy playing with and spoiling the dog without the ultimate responsibility for their dog's safe and productive entry into society. Of course, the human motivation is love, but love absent education can selfishly deprive a dog of a good foundation which will liberate him to enjoy his family and freedom to the utmost.

We remember a couple in their late 30s who had two small children and Jasper, a large dog who had begun to snap at the kids as well as visitors, particularly when they approached the wife. In listening to the details, we realized the dog was very bonded to the female owner and vice versa—which is a good thing—but she had created few if any rules for this dog to follow, and she thought of him as one of the children. Her husband worked long hours and left most of the dog's care to his wife.

As a consequence, the dog tolerated the husband but wouldn't particularly obey him either. Once Jasper snapped at one of the children, and the husband attempted to take the dog by the collar to move him away. Jasper growled at him. The man was startled and let go of the collar. The only person Jasper never threatened was the wife.

This was a delicate situation in the husband's eyes because on some level he knew he was not present enough in the home to just take charge and make changes. His wife already felt neglected, and he was reluctant to tell her what she should do. How do we know all this? Very often dog trainers become marriage counselors, therapists, or life coaches in the course of doing their job. The most personal things tend to leak out when discussing home life as it applies to the family and dog. We knew what was going on in the home because they told us. We were honored they would confide in us even though it was difficult and emotional for them. But it was helpful because it explained so much.

The husband wanted to be a good provider and was very successful, but he worked too much and felt guilty for neglecting his wife and children. The wife was as understanding as she could manage but naturally had a certain resentment, which she expressed at our consultation. And who could blame her? She ran the household largely on her own and was raising the children, but she found it truly difficult to create rules for the dog, the one creature in the house she thought she could love without having to sacrifice yet more of her emotions.

We laid out a program to explain to these clients the structure and simple rules their children and dog needed to become safer in their home. Jasper had not yet bitten anyone. However, his behavior was beginning to deteriorate further, and this worried the couple. But the wife really struggled to accept that the same concepts she was applying to her parenting of the children were also critical to her "parenting" of the dog.

We gave them both homework. The husband was to walk Jasper daily, an important bonding element, giving the dog much-needed exercise and his wife a much-needed assist. Both were to stop letting the dog sleep in bed with them until Jasper had made—and maintained—a behavioral turnaround. We also asked the wife to tell Jasper to go lie down on his dog bed when she wanted to cuddle her children, teaching him that he didn't own all her personal space.

These procedures gave the family a structured pathway forward to improve Jasper's behavior and keep the people in his life safe. Sometimes, overindulging the dog may actually endanger a beloved pet. In this instance, the good news is that

Jasper was willing to change his ways when the owners clearly indicated new and better expectations. By sticking to the plan and following instructions, Jasper's owners gave him the gift of love *with* rules.

The nature of dogs is such that they willingly follow human guidelines if only those will be laid out for them in a way they can understand. Rules should be fair to the dog while we simultaneously provide for their physical and psychological needs, all of which we will discuss in more detail in upcoming chapters. But if you are to train your dog, first you must understand a bit about how he thinks. If you are a good Pack Leader, your dog can be a good pack follower. If you do not lead, not only can he not follow, but he will think the pack has elected him leader to make critical choices for all of you. Most dogs who take on this role do not become aggressive; they merely act out in naughty ways. But many forms of mischief can be dangerous for the dogs and even the entire family: chewing and ingesting clothing or turning on bathtub faucets and even the handle on the gas stove! We have hundreds of case histories in which owners failed to provide proper leadership and exercise for their dogs and suffered the consequences of completely avoidable problem behavior.

What do we actually seek to accomplish by training the dog? Before we even begin the process, we have a series of goals in mind—some philosophical, others quite concrete. All these goals then fit together like the pieces of a jigsaw puzzle to make one larger picture: you and your dog doing whatever it is you both like best.

For active adults, the picture may be hiking through a snow-covered forest in the mountains of Colorado with an off-leash husky. The dog is romping on the trail but remaining in sight, occasionally coming to sit at your side, allowing other hikers and dogs to pass. For others, the picture may consist of a shaggy mixed breed lying by your side as you sip coffee. You are reading news on the patio of your favorite coffee shop while your dog calmly accepts the admiring glances of strangers. Or maybe you're looking out of your kitchen window into the backyard, watching your yellow Labrador chasing a ball and playing with your children on a summer afternoon.

Philosophically, our ultimate goal is to liberate the dog from conflict and nagging. If you frequently must tell your dog that he's doing wrong—Stop! Quiet! Leave it! No! Come here! Go away!—then the basis of your relationship has slipped into the negative. Surely your dog will know he's doing wrong because dogs have evolved to "figure out" this confusing species called human and to understand when we are pleased or displeased. But expressing frustration with a dog's behavior is not necessarily educational. In other words, he may get the general idea that you don't like what he's doing, but he probably won't learn what you want him to do instead. And this is critical. Real education consists far more of "let's do this" so you'll need far less of "don't do that."

The opposite of conflict is harmony. This is precisely what we envision when we begin to train a dog, and we hope you will do the same. Imagine how much better you will feel when you no longer have to micromanage your dog by constantly scolding or issuing orders. A good dog does what you tell him to do when you give a command because of the relationship you have established. You say sit, and he sits. Good dog. What could be better than that?

We're here to inspire you and to assure you that it can get better than that. Our hope is that, trained with our method and using the exercises and goals we set out for you, you will help your dog become first a good dog, yes. But optimally we will be setting him up to become something more: a great dog.

A good dog does as you ask. A great dog offers good behavior appropriate to the moment before you ask. Here's an example. Marc's beloved Doberman came to him at 1 year of age, a rescue already saddled with the unfortunate name of Diablo. When Marc first adopted him, the dog was 87 pounds of wild. He pulled hard on the leash, scarfed food off the counters, and refused to come when called unless he was hungry and food bribes were offered. As his training progressed, Diablo first learned to comply with obedience exercises and commands. As he became better trained and more reliable at obeying the basic commands necessary for his safety, Marc taught Diablo something new, something elusive and hard to describe in words. Marc taught his dog the value of a relationship—that the more Diablo would mind meld with him, the more the dog got what he truly wanted.

Diablo loved three things above all else: running, playing with other dogs, and close physical contact with his Pack Leaders. As soon as the dog understood that *come* means come without hesitation, regardless of distractions, Marc and his partner were

When dog and owner truly understand one another's needs, a sort of mind meld brings them closer

able to let Diablo run on Chicago's dog-friendly beach. Because he learned polite leash manners, Diablo was given the opportunity for controlled, beneficial pulling. Diablo often pulled Marc's partner, who wore in-line skates, for 10 miles along Chicago's lakefront, from North Avenue Beach to the Shedd Aquarium and back.

And because Diablo learned to leave the kitchen counters alone, he was permitted to lay his head in Marc's lap whenever Marc did paperwork at the table. Both of them loved that, and all of it is *good dog* stuff. That being said, if Marc put food on the table, Diablo would not merely want to rest his head on Marc's lap.

Naturally, he was tempted to sniff at the plate, which was at eye level for him. That violation of good manners caused Marc to take Diablo just outside the kitchen and put him in a down-stay right at the threshold. The dog would comply with his down-stay, but sorrowfully.

After a while, something interesting happened. At first Marc wasn't even aware of it, but eventually he noticed that he was eating a plate of food and Diablo's head wasn't on his lap. He looked and saw that the dog had voluntarily vacated and lain down at the threshold of the kitchen. But since he had volunteered for that down, Marc no longer needed to insist he maintain it. In other words, because Diablo chose to lie down outside the kitchen, he was free to get up and move around other parts of the house at will. Furthermore, Marc soon noticed that as soon as he put the plates on the table, Diablo would move back and lie himself down at the threshold of the kitchen without second thought. Diablo had become a great dog, going way beyond mere compliance with obedience commands. Because Marc so often used those commands to provide Diablo with his favorite things, the dog opted into the relationship in a profound way, looking for opportunities to give what was needed before he was asked. It takes two to tango.

A dog is happiest when allowed to reach his full potential. But what does that really mean?

It certainly doesn't mean spending a majority of his time outside tied to a tree. That is unacceptable on all counts. But is it enough for life to consist of barking at the neighbor's dog when outside behind a fence, alternating with barking at the mailman through the windows when inside the house? This is life for millions and millions of our dogs. Granted, they're happy to see family when we come home, they adore playing with the children or other pets, and they love to share the sofa as you watch TV. They're lucky because they receive regular veterinary care and good food.

But is it enough?

Certainly, some dogs thrive on a routine where they rarely ever leave the property. But most will find far more fulfillment if they can behave well enough in the car to go on road trips with you and if they're trustworthy off the leash in places where that is legal and safe. Have you ever dreamed of taking your dog to work? Hiking with your dog loose in the woods? Watching him play at an off-leash dog park, secure in the knowledge you can call him away from any trouble that might erupt at the far end of the park?

If you can dream those things, you can achieve them. We're certain of that because we have done it over and over again with our own dogs. In addition, through our boarding school programs and books, we've helped thousands of clients get the same results with their dogs. Using an e-collar through the method we present will turn your dream into reality and enhance the relationship you share with your dog. The trick will be to envision the dream and then follow a pathway to achieve it. Our method makes this possible, and we're going to teach it to you here in a very sequential, thorough way. We simply want you to understand that you can be aiming, and training, for a higher goal than for a sit-stay or any traditional obedience exercise. You can be training for a life of freedom, understanding, and relating to your dog.

Diablo was a friendly dog. Many people mistakenly believe Doberman pinschers to be aggressive guard dogs. Although the breed does possess an instinct to guard their people, most owners would agree their dogs are big babies, happier to meet strangers than to challenge them. Diablo certainly fell into that category. Marc lived in urban Chicago during much of the dog's life span, and if he was driving, Diablo could usually be found snoozing in the back seat. At red lights, newspaper vendors might approach the car, and beggars would not only approach but knock on the windows. Diablo might open one eye at such moments, but he could rarely be bothered to object to strangers walking near his car.

Very late one night, Marc left his home for Midway airport to pick up a friend. As he pulled out of the garage, he stopped and went back into the house to get Diablo. It would be nice to have the company and Diablo enjoyed a car ride, Marc thought.

That last-minute decision—made possible by motivational dog training—probably saved Marc's life.

Forty minutes later, with Diablo lazily reclined in the back seat, Marc stopped for a red light on a deserted Chicago street. Not a car in sight. Suddenly two men with guns rushed the car from opposite sides. One came toward the driver's door, the other toward the passenger's door. Diablo, normally unconcerned about people

Well-behaved dogs get to spend more quality time with their family

getting close to the vehicle, not only noticed but objected. Loudly and viciously. While Marc sat momentarily frozen with confusion, Diablo rose up from his hidden position on the back seat and tried to break through the back windows on either side. Roaring with a sort of bark he had never made before, he caused both carjackers to jump away from the vehicle, giving Marc the instant he needed to speed away through the red light.

A good dog does what you ask. A great dog does it without being asked. And sometimes a great dog may know what to do even when you do not.

Naturally, we're not downplaying obedience command training. The monks wrote an entire book on it some years ago. Obedience skills are important. Yet our goals in training the dog are multiple. First, we want a dog who comes when called and who sits when asked. We want a dog who lies down and stays when we need him to stay. We want a dog who walks politely on the leash, right by our side, willing to ignore distractions like people, other dogs, and birds. We even want a dog who will go lie down on his dog bed and wait there when we point.

Moving beyond commands, however, comes a dog who knows how to follow the reasonable rules you set forth, and most of all, simply knows how to be polite. Dogs with etiquette will invariably be free to spend more time with their owners than those who are happily ignorant of how to behave in different situations. If your dog knows the rules of civilized behavior in and out of your home, you won't often need to issue actual commands, let alone stern ones. Rules tend to vary from home to home but usually include such things as not barking to excess, leaving food alone on counters or tables, allowing guests to enter the home without jumping, and so forth.

To sum it up, in this book we will seek to train the dog to competence with commands. Moreover, we'll teach him how to be polite and to anticipate our needs. But critically, we'll also teach you how to anticipate and meet your dog's needs so that you may enable him to fulfill his part of the relationship. We will do all of the above using our method of dog training, which as you know incorporates the use of the gentlest new technology available, the modern e-collar, or remote training collar as we often call it.

Finally, the magic is not in the tool. It is in your hands, your mind, your dog's mind, and in your mutual relationship. Although the e-collar is an incredibly useful tool—and in our technique a highly nuanced one—the magic does not reside in technology. That is why we will train with an eye toward producing a trained dog who understands what you need, shares your life collaboratively, and can ultimately be weaned off regular use of the e-collar.

That is not to say you won't find it useful throughout your dog's life, such as when he's off leash. There is great comfort and security in knowing you can go off-leash hiking but still reinforce a long-distance recall off high distractions such as deer. You may find an easy "rule reminder system" very handy with a houseful of guests and food during parties or holidays. Still, our ultimate goal is a structured and gradually reduced reliance on any tool other than the relationship we intend to build. Eventually, you'll be able to fade the e-collar for most everyday situations when your dog is in the house or being walked on leash.

Our signature training method helps the bond of trust become even stronger

CHAPTER 3

Addressing the Controversy

Can a loving dog owner train her dog using an e-collar, and can that process be gentle? The answer is a resounding yes. We know that for a fact because we've been doing it for years now. There are two primary reasons why modern e-collars can generously contribute to the training of modern pets. The first reason is new technology. Since the mid-1990s most aspects of technology have modernized, miniaturized, and radically improved. Cell phones started out as giant bricks that were carried around in their own briefcases. They had one function only: voice calls. Compare that to the small, sophisticated smartphones of today.

So it has also been with e-collars. They started out in the 1960s as big, clunky collars designed only to punish car chasers and chicken killers or to be used with hunting dogs in the field, where off-leash control was imperative. Now the modern e-collar can deliver a barely perceptible signal to the dog, one which he can feel, but lightly. In fact, the feeling is so delicate that we ask all of our clients to put the collar on their own hand so they may understand how gentle the sensation is that their dogs detect and respond to. Just like dogs, all people are different when it comes to feeling an e-collar pulse. What one person definitively feels, another person may not even detect. This is why e-collars have variable levels: so that we can always find what a dog will feel without causing discomfort.

The second reason e-collars now take their place alongside other useful dog training tools is related to methodology. We use our highly refined and time-tested method because it is an approach that quickly makes sense to dogs and the owners who have been exposed to it.

In our last book, *Let Dogs Be Dogs*, we wrote extensively about your dog's natural desire for you to be his Pack Leader, a term popularized by the monks in the 1970s. The training method we will detail for you in this book is well structured, so that you will be able to re-create it at home with your own dog. It's gentle and we believe you will be surprised at your rapid progress once you begin the simple and straightforward lesson plans. This training program will help you become the Pack Leader your dog craves.

Of course, nothing good comes without the "less good" side of things. Therefore, some of the cheaper e-collars our clients sometimes purchase on their own actually make us shudder. That's because they are incapable of delivering the sort of subtle sensations we require as a hallmark of our approach. *Not all e-collars are alike.* Some are poorly made and will make most dogs decidedly uncomfortable.

It's not just about technology, though. Methodology must be developed to take advantage of newly developed equipment. Remember, e-collars don't train dogs. People train dogs. The e-collar is just an inanimate tool until a skilled trainer breathes life into a relationship with the dog by using the collar in a particular fashion. Moreover, just because good technology exists doesn't necessarily mean that all methods are alike or that all are gentle. We have seen a few trainers promoting methods on social media using e-collars that make us as uncomfortable as we suppose the dogs they are training must feel. Others do a creditable job. But let us make this assertion: good e-collars matched with good training techniques will produce good training. Good training produces well-behaved dogs who are confident and unafraid and whose personalities are intact, and indeed, allowed to flourish.

It's that simple.

Regardless of training techniques and tools, some owners are afraid that training will depress or rob their dog of her personality. Nothing could be further from the truth, at least when we're talking about *good* dog training. Good dog training teaches a dog to control some of her impulses to behave wildly, destructively, or downright dangerously. But it also teaches a dog that her owner will make ample provision for her to exercise her body and her brain so she will no longer feel compelled to act out in wild, unmanageable ways. Think of it this way: today's better educational

Training is intended to liberate the dog rather than suppress her energy and joy

processes don't rob children of personality. The "spare the rod and spoil the child" schools of the past may well have done so—for both children and dogs—but that is far from the case today. Similarly, we know from personal experience that your dog's personality will thrive and find delightful new forms of expression when you can trust her to come when called and walk politely on a leash.

An old-time dog trainer from Louisiana, Dick Russell, had many folksy aphorisms. In discussing dog training equipment, Dick's favorite saying was, "It's not the tool. It's the fool." What he meant was that dog training tools were not bad in and of themselves. It is uneducated or impatient people who are prone to making mistakes when using certain tools, mistakes that needlessly upset or even hurt a dog. Our intent with our method and with this book is to educate you so that you can select the best tools for the job and train your dog in a manner that will please you both. We think you'll find that your dog is unafraid, her behavior is improving, and your own confidence has grown.

A Therapeutic Touch

We understand that many people haven't had very pleasant experiences with electricity in general, and this probably causes an instinctive sort of worry to dog lovers when they consider an e-collar. If, for example, you so much as forget to use a dryer sheet in the laundry, you may get a really unpleasant zap when separating a pair of nylon socks. Some people worry that the e-collar feeling might be more like the zap from the socks or worse. But don't forget that low levels of electricity have been used therapeutically in physical therapy and doctor's offices for decades through transcutaneous electrical nerve stimulation (TENS). The machine stimulates nerves to help heal damaged muscles with a pulse that many people find pleasant. Ironically, the stimulation from an e-collar used in our practice is lighter than that from a TENS unit, yet no one would object to its value.

Also a bit ironic is how underground electronic dog fences have become so commonplace that the early controversy about them has largely disappeared in a sea of happy suburban dog owners. Millions of pet lovers are able to give their dogs fuller use of the yard because a buried wire around the perimeter communicates with an electronic fence collar worn by the dog. A training process teaches the dog that he will receive first a warning tone if he gets too close to the perimeter. If the dog ignores that tone and gets closer, he will receive an electric stimulation. These dogs are essentially being "trained" by an automated e-collar.

If you were to put a fence collar on your hand and walk out of the yard, you would call it an uncomfortable shock. The stimulation delivered by those millions of fence collars is markedly higher than what we do or recommend in our e-collar training. Why is it that angry coalitions of "all-positive" dog trainers try to ban e-collars when many of those dog trainers have clients who successfully use electronic fences? There is an inconsistency here. Simply put, selling food-based training is easier, even when real-world results are lacking. As Winston Churchill memorably said, "However beautiful the strategy, you should occasionally look at the results." It's also understandable why e-collars may be viewed with concern. Remember, we too were initially prejudiced against any method using e-collars simply because we had not seen the new technology, and even when we did, we saw it being used poorly.

What is poor e-collar training? It can be divided into two major subgroups.

First, you have training that just isn't very effective. The word "training" in our thinking can be used interchangeably with the word "education." Unfortunately, some training is not very educational at all because it does not teach the dog *what to do;* rather, it focuses on correcting the dog for doing wrong things. In other words, it only teaches the dog what *not* to do. The main thrust of this type of training is avoidance, using the collar as an aversive. While teaching the dog to keep his nose out of the kitchen trash isn't a bad thing, it certainly doesn't bring you closer to hiking in the woods or being able to bring the dog to soccer practice. Aversive training is basic and limited. Also, people tend to overdo it. In teaching the dog to stay out of the trash, you might accidentally send the wrong message, scaring the dog and making her afraid to even enter the kitchen. An increasingly large percentage of our training clients mention that they have purchased an e-collar but are not using it because they quickly realized they needed more information to use it well. That leads owners to trainers, many of whom are skilled and patient with the e-collar.

Patience
and reward
are critical
components of
reliable training

Unfortunately, the flip side of that coin means that some training is impatient and focuses more on quick results rather than a measured, enjoyable process. While that can be true of any human–dog interaction, it is especially easy to overdo it when power tools are involved. An unskilled or impatient owner or trainer can cause discomfort for the dog, accidentally teaching the wrong lesson.

We remember a couple who came to us with Lucy, a very affectionate pit bull. She had been completely sociable for her first 3 years with both people and dogs. In fact, she was a legend at the local dog park, a perfect ambassador for her breed. One day a cocker spaniel repeatedly attacked Lucy. She put up with it over and over until she had had enough. With one swift move, Lucy pinned the aggressive little spaniel to the ground, releasing it when Lucy's owners peeled her off. There wasn't even a scratch on that cocker, but naturally Lucy's owners hustled her out of the dog park at once.

Because they were a bit traumatized by that event, they didn't bring Lucy back to the park for several days. When they did, they entered nervously, making sure the cocker wasn't there. The first time a dog came up behind Lucy, surprising her a little bit, the nervous owners yelled at Lucy and pulled her away. Within a few days Lucy naturally started to become paranoid that all dogs had suddenly turned bad. After all, she had that unfortunate experience with the cocker, and her owners were jumpy and even panicky around dogs ever since.

So Lucy began to growl at dogs who got close to them on walks. This made her owners even more nervous. They bought a cheap e-collar and used it poorly. Of course, this was completely unintentional. Lucy's owners loved her; they just didn't know better. And what they did could just as easily have been done by an unskilled trainer. With no preparation, they waited until Lucy was growling at a dog before they pushed the button, using a painful level on a poorly designed collar.

Did Lucy draw the conclusion they wished? That she should stop growling at dogs? That dogs are safe? That her own behavior was the problem? No. The law of unintended consequences took over. Lucy figured that somehow the other dog bit her even though it was 6 feet away. Soon she began growling at 15 feet. The owners repeated the same sequence, and within a few weeks poor Lucy was going ballistic when she laid eyes on any dog, regardless of distance. Eventually the owners had to walk Lucy at 4 a.m. to avoid dogs.

They were constantly nervous, so they came to see us. Out of sight of dogs, we taught Lucy that a gentle tap (pressing one of the buttons) from a good e-collar meant she should stop whatever she was doing and turn around to look at us, even if there was a blowing leaf to investigate. In upcoming chapters we will thoroughly detail this process. Once she was prepared to understand that concept, we introduced dogs into the situation, but from very far away. Then we just taught the lesson again. Forget that dog; turn and follow us. Eventually we were able to close up the gap and get calmly close to dogs again. It took a while, but once they could walk Lucy again, quality of life soared for the entire family, including the dog.

It's not the tool. It's the fool. Our clients certainly weren't fools. They were loving and highly educated people. But you know what we mean. Unfortunately, the owners weren't educated about e-collars, and they did what seemed logical to them. But for great dog training, regardless of the tool, human logic must meld with *dog logic* to work out for the best.

As a training tool, a proper e-collar is neither good nor bad in and of itself. It's simply a tool to be either used artfully or not. Although we will analyze what makes a good e-collar, one you should buy to use with your dog, the magic isn't in the tool. An e-collar is just a plastic device filled with circuits and a battery. The magic will come from *you* as you apply the technique we will carefully lay out for you. Indeed, our method is a technique comprising precisely what you do with that e-collar; what you do with your leash, voice, and body; and what you do with your commands, treats, and rewards.

We realize the internet is chock-full of wild rumors and so-called science-backed claims that condemn a very wide spectrum of dog training tools of which the e-collar is just one. We won't waste any time on those here or on the proponents of so-called "all-positive" dog training, which soundly condemns anything that isn't 100 percent reward based. The limitations of that approach are so obvious that most owners who go through it are eventually relieved to find a solution to their dog problems which, yes, involves reward and fun, but which does not entirely rely on food bribery. The

Used correctly, the e-collar is a tool that can unleash a dog's potential

squirrel will always be more important to the dog than the cookie. What the true believers in "all-positive" training lack in effectiveness they make up for with zealous condemnation of any other approach, regardless of its kindness and efficacy.

Since the 1970s, the Monks of New Skete have shared their philosophies and training methods through their books. Starting with *How to Be Your Dog's Best Friend* and then continuing with *The Art of Raising a Puppy*, the monks have assisted millions of owners in enjoying fuller and better relationships with their dogs. Marc Goldberg has also been training dogs since the 1970s and coauthored *Let Dogs Be Dogs*. Together, your authors not only train client dogs, but for years have also been training the trainers. Hundreds of professional dog trainers have taken our how-to workshops, and those trainers have gone on to assist thousands of their dog-owning clients. We hope to continue helping countless dogs and families be happy with one another.

Dogs are remarkably open-minded. They respond to most any method of dog training, absorbing the lessons taught. The problem, of course, is that owners and trainers sometimes teach the dog an unintended lesson. For example, if we teach the dog that coming when called will produce a treat, we will get good compliance from a food-motivated dog who is not especially distracted when we call her. Further, even if we teach her that coming when called will produce a treat, dogs—a domesticated version of wolves, complex problem-solving predators—quickly deduce that responding to interesting distractions is more gratifying than any food reward. Thus, we get inconsistent and unreliable training results if we rely on food as the only motivation for coming when called.

Trainers call the *come* command a recall. It is nice when you can call your dog and she recalls from the bedroom to you at the front door so you can go for the evening walk. And if you allow your dog to go out for a quick potty in your fenced backyard, we're sure the dog normally comes back in when you call. But ask yourself, must you literally wave treats to get your dog's attention? If there is a squirrel or another dog in sight, do you have to call repeatedly and raise your voice? Must you sometimes go out into the yard and physically herd or corral your dog to get her inside?

A dog who recalls most of the time is pretty good. But pretty good isn't the same as *really* good, and it certainly isn't safe when you're not behind that fence. You don't have a reliable recall until you can recall your dog off squirrels, rabbits, birds, kids, cats, dogs, flying monkeys, and UFOs.

Who doesn't want that?

Our style has always been to educate the dog, giving her clarity on what we are asking her to do, and how and when to do it. We also show her what praise and, yes, even sometimes what treats she will earn for doing it. We use common sense and benign reminders to clarify that, although we intend for the commands to be more fun than drudgery, they are still not optional.

When we first began to experiment with the new and improved e-collar technology, we quickly discovered that it had more potential than ever before. But there was no clear pathway forward, no book, no guide, and certainly no good and patient experience to emulate. Therefore, we had to feel our way through the learning process,

Calm, quiet praise tells the dog that she's doing the right thing

experimenting and developing a method as we learned more. Luckily, we had decades of experience on which to build. This was important because it allowed us to quickly read a dog's attitude and immediately understand if we were seeing discomfort or joy, worry or confidence, concern or legitimate learning. Over the years, we refined our process until we could routinely—and more quickly than ever before—train a happy, confident dog to mind his manners and be reliable under distracting circumstances.

When you are the passenger in a car with a skilled driver behind the wheel, you're not even aware that the driver is engaged in the mechanics of steering, braking, and accelerating. On the other hand, we've all experienced the nervous, untalented driver who does everything roughly, making us nervous and uncomfortable. Shall we blame the car? No. It is an inanimate object and in fact is a marvel of

Modern technology allows us to safely enjoy a good old-fashioned romp in the park

engineering, enhancing our lives enormously when used correctly. And so are the modern e-collars that we use in our daily work, teaching dogs to enjoy freedom of movement and yet remain safe.

An Approach for the 21st Century . . . With These Provisos

We believe this book is very timely and very much needed because e-collars are a fast-growing segment within the rapidly expanding pet market. They are not going away. The overall pet market is now over $70 billion annually. As pets have become less like property and more like family members, the number of pets kept as well as the dollars spent on them has been growing fast. More pet dogs and more money spent, combined with more and better technology, means that electronic training products have skyrocketed in availability. At last check, searching for "electronic dog collar" on Amazon returned over 1,000 results for different products, some useful and some not so much. You can also purchase e-collars in most popular big box stores in and out of the pet store segment. Name a large chain retailer, and chances are you can purchase an e-collar from them, either off the shelf or through their website. Greg Van Curen, owner of E-Collar Technologies, a collar developer and manufacturer of an e-collar we can recommend, estimates that over 1 million e-collars are being sold per year as of 2019.

The genie is out of the bottle. Technology is here, and it will not be stuffed back into a time capsule and buried. Therefore, it is high time that loving, responsible dog owners learned a technique to use this technology in a way that serves the relationship rather than disturbs it. That is what we have for you here with our method.

We know this book will stir up controversy. At the same time, the vast majority of the monks' and Marc's dog training clients will either not understand what all the fuss is about or have themselves become converts. That's because when you take a good-quality e-collar and use it to gently educate a dog with our technique, you'll see a happy dog, one who can even enjoy both the learning process and the end result. Our method is not something you do *to* your dog. It is something you do *with* your dog.

Daily walks are a critical component of a dog's routine, both for us at the monastery and for you in your neighborhood. They allow a dog to experience a range of instincts.

Understanding What Makes Your Dog Tick

Take a walk with us at New Skete with two of our German shepherds, Fuller and Hannah, who are both a little over 2 years of age. It is a crisp, windy spring day, and we are hiking along the empty, mile-long private road that is our driveway to let the dogs frolic and exercise before they rest a bit and then have their late afternoon meal. Birch, white pine, and maple trees line the road, and the dogs weave in and out around us, scenting the grass along either side of the road, playing happily with each other, then returning to scenting the ground as they move forward down the road. The dogs are delighting in each other when a strong gust of wind passes over us and a tree branch cracks and falls to the ground far off to our right. Hannah startles and darts quickly away from the direction of the sound, hackles raised, unsure of the cause of the noise. Fuller, on the other hand, stands his ground and glares intently in the direction of the tree. His hackles are raised as well, and he utters a low growl. We quickly reassure both dogs and keep moving forward. Soon Fuller and Hannah are back to the business of their walk, having forgotten about the momentary disruption.

Since the monastery has about 500 acres of land, there is an abundance of wildlife on the property: deer, bear, wild turkey, pheasant, porcupine, and raccoon, not to mention squirrels, chipmunks, rabbits, and other small creatures. While ordinarily wildlife avoids the approach of the dogs, occasionally they will encounter a surprise leap from the brush and a quick chase will ensue until we call them back. And so it is on this walk, as a large doe suddenly jumps from the tree line across the road and continues away with remarkable grace and speed. Fuller and Hannah don't hesitate. They immediately chase after the doe down the road. However, they do ease up after about 20 feet and redirect their attention back to us in conjunction with light taps we have been giving on the e-collar from the moment they started running. Once they have returned to us, we praise them warmly and pet them while they lean into us, obviously enjoying the affection. But as we continue the walk, it is apparent that they still are interested in the now-departed doe. They follow the scent of the path it took and look longingly at the woods where it entered, tempted to follow. Nevertheless, they respond to our commands and continue on with us, and the rest of the walk takes place without any further incident.

Such a walk is not that remarkable for us at the level to which our dogs are trained, even though we realize that many dog owners would jump at the chance to have wonderful adventures like this safely. Yet walks with our dogs often transpire in this way, and at first glance one may wonder why we would spend time even considering the incident. However, what such a walk reveals is the manifestation of instinctual characteristics in the dog that have evolved over time and which express themselves naturally in everyday life. They have helped them survive and thrive as a species for millennia. Broadly speaking, these instinctive behaviors can be divided into three general categories of drives: prey, defense, and pack. Each drive will be found to varying degrees in every dog. Knowing this is important because the ways the drives express themselves in individual behaviors will determine a dog's basic temperament, his unique personality, and the way he views the world around him. It will also suggest appropriate ways to work with the dog in training.

Understanding the Drives

Prey drive is the instinct most connected with the dog's survival as a hunter, as when Fuller and Hannah chased after the doe. Historically, dogs survived by being predators: they hunted and chased after their prey, killed it, and then ate it. Without this instinct, the dog would never have survived in the wild. The factors

Even puppies have prey drive: this youngster has spied a frog

that trigger prey drive are motion, sound, and scent, which then result in a variety of behaviors: total sense alertness (sight, hearing, smell), chasing, high-pitched barking, pouncing, jumping up, shaking, carrying, killing, eating, and the like. Dogs are simply hardwired for such behaviors by virtue of this drive. Even today, when for the most part dogs don't have to hunt, we still observe prey drive readily when a dog chases after a squirrel in the backyard or runs a cat up the tree, but most especially in play behaviors such as fetch or when dogs chase each other around an open space. It is easy to see how much dogs enjoy acting out of this instinct, and dogs that are properly conditioned can stay in this mode for long periods of time. This is one of the reasons why dogs come home from doggy daycare tired and easily able to chill out.

Defense drive is the dog's instinct for self-preservation and survival. We saw it when Fuller and Hannah each responded differently to the crash of the tree limb. It manifests itself in one of two seemingly contradictory behaviors: fight or flight. For this reason, it is more nuanced than prey drive in dogs because the same trigger that makes one dog aggressive in defending itself elicits avoidance behavior in another, especially in younger, less confident dogs. Fight behaviors tend to strengthen naturally as dogs mature, though we see the development of both sides of defense drive in litters of puppies. Puppies will ritually play fight with each other and learn from the interactions when to assert dominance and submission. This also helps identify individual personalities in the litter and each pup's position in the social hierarchy. Depending on individual personality and ordinary socializing, as dogs mature we see clearer indications of how each dog manifests this drive. More dominant dogs will express body language signaling self-confidence: in approaching other dogs, for example, they will stare at them and then "stand tall" over them while remaining absolutely still beside them. Hackles, tail, and ears will be elevated and ears will be moving forward, waiting for a sign of submission from the other dog. In the case of two dominant dogs, such an encounter can escalate into a fight if not interrupted. Dogs strong in defense drive will move toward new and unfamiliar situations and objects, again with hackles raised. At the sound of a doorbell, they will bark aggressively and move toward the door. Often they will guard their food and toys, and they can try to control space by positioning themselves in such a way as to make the owner walk around them.

Less confident dogs express defense drive by avoiding or fleeing situations in which the dog is uncomfortable or unsure of itself. While such a dog will raise its hackles the length of its body in these cases, its tail will be tucked and ears more flattened as it moves away from whatever is threatening it. Such "flight"-oriented dogs often don't like meeting or being touched by strangers and will avoid other novel situations due to their lack of confidence. Their modus operandi is to flee from whatever would threaten them.

Dogs are highly social creatures, and pack drive is what governs behaviors linked with being part of a group, or pack, as well as those associated with reproduction, such as licking, mounting, and various types of courting behaviors. We saw it manifest in Fuller and Hannah during their walk as they playfully stayed close to us while interacting with each other, as well as when they returned to us after briefly chasing the doe. As pack animals, dogs are highly sensitive to social hierarchy and the rules that promote the smooth functioning of the pack. This means that dogs naturally are oriented toward collaborating with a consistent, good-natured leader to maintain good order in the pack. Good training promotes this, and we see the flowering of pack drive through physical contact, play, companionship, verbal praise, and learning to be attentive to the guidance of the Pack Leader. It's not hard to see how a dog who is strong in pack drive will want to be with you. She will follow you around the house and seems happiest while in your company. Such dogs don't like being alone for long periods of time, and they love being petted and groomed. Dogs that are high in pack drive are a joy to be around; they are highly trainable, affectionate, and elicit from their human companions some of the noblest characteristics in human nature.

Drives and Personality

All dogs manifest aspects of each drive to some degree, and the ways the drives integrate and express themselves in the behavior of the individual dog reveal her unique personality. Nevertheless, individual drives can be brought to the surface in each dog through skillful training. At our training facilities we try to draw out each drive in a constructive way that allows dogs to interact with each other gracefully. Balanced training aspires to a balanced and appropriate expression of each drive to the extent possible in each dog. To enhance prey drive, for example, we use motion games such as fetch or chase to bring out the drive in a controlled manner. We bring out defense drive through a sharp voice and other techniques that interrupt behavior, which we will discuss in greater detail as we move forward in the book. And we bring out pack drive by physical affection, verbal praise, judicious use of treats, and positive body language.

While there is no doubt that particular breeds will tend to emphasize particular drives as a result of selective breeding, it is also the case that there will be individual dogs in each breed that are less normative. At New Skete, for example, the German

Using a technique we will teach you, Brother Christopher backs away from the dog . . .

. . . engaging her pack drive so that she wants to come to him

shepherd breeding program has been in existence for approximately 50 years. While many of the dogs that we've bred reflect the general characteristics of the German shepherd dog—dogs that are high in working abilities related to hunting and protective behavior—there also have been some dogs that are clearly high in pack drive but not so much in either defense or prey drive. This is one reason why individual dogs can be placed in different types of living situations: some dogs will be ideally suited for active, athletic families, while others will do better in lower-key environments, such as with an older, less active couple.

Switching Drives

From this discussion, it should be apparent that dogs are never exclusively in one drive. They shift from one drive to another in a very natural way, depending on the circumstances. Our job as owners and companions is to help them shift drives appropriately. For example, picture yourself playing fetch with your dog in your fenced-in yard (prey). In the midst of the game, a delivery truck pulls up the driveway and your dog runs to the fence, barking (defense). You call your dog, and he comes trotting back to you. You praise him warmly as he moves into a down-stay beside you (pack). This is what happens in training. We teach our dogs to shift from one drive to another based on context and our command, so that we are able to function as a team. There are so many applications of this principle in daily life that it will be important for you to know how to switch your dog from one drive to another. An ordinary walk in which one minute you are walking your dog calmly with a loose leash may quickly change into a sudden lunge as a chipmunk crosses the sidewalk. Your dog has gone from pack drive to full-blown prey drive instantaneously. To get him back into pack drive, you have to be able to interrupt him by going through defense drive which, because of training, he is able to respond to. By understanding what drive your dog happens to be in at any one time, you'll be able to communicate with him more meaningfully and fairly.

Every dog is unique. What makes dog training such a fascinating profession for both of us is the opportunity to work with a wide variety of dogs, to become real students of *Canis familiaris*. Over the years we have had the privilege of training thousands of dogs from well over 100 registered breeds. Training dogs never gets boring because each dog has his own personality, and while individual dog breeds possess general behavioral characteristics, within each breed you will find individual dogs that don't fit the stereotypical breed profile: an unusually dominant golden retriever, a highly social and affectionate Akita, a laid-back Doberman pinscher, a couch-potato Jack Russell terrier, and so on. Because of this, it is vital for a good trainer to have a solid understanding of both general breed characteristics and the particular ways they express themselves in individual dogs. Not all dogs can be trained in exactly the same way. Training becomes an art when you are able to adapt your particular approach to the individual dog with whom you are working. We remember a client who brought a year-old Labrador retriever, Maggie, for training. The owner had adopted Maggie from a shelter, and while ordinarily Labs are very sociable and quick learners, Maggie was just the opposite. She was extremely shy and fearful, and this affected the way she learned. When she first came to New Skete, she wanted nothing to do with other dogs, and in her initial training sessions, it proved challenging simply to get her out of her pen and teach her how to walk on leash without anxiety. While it is extremely likely that Maggie spent her first months of life in anything but an enriched environment, it also seems likely that she was genetically disposed toward shy behavior. The challenge for us was to reduce her more submissive defense drive and bring out Maggie's pack drive to the extent possible during the time she was with us. This meant that we had to approach her training in a way that respected Maggie's unique personality and which concentrated initially on establishing a trusting relationship with her before beginning more formal training in earnest. We built up her pack drive by introducing her to frequent walks, tethering her throughout the day with one of the trainers, and using high-value treats and warm praise to help motivate her. We taught her how to play tug in a manner that helped build her self-confidence, and finally we used low-level e-collar work to focus her attention. Over a couple of weeks, she responded in a way that was gratifying. But the key point is that, had we trained her like one of our boisterous and self-confident German shepherds, the results would not have been as positive. So much depends on the personality of the individual dog and how we balance the drives.

While all of the preceding is true, it shouldn't be surprising that, for our purposes in this book, we will be focusing primarily on reinforcing pack drive and how to use that to its fullest advantage in your relationship with your dog. One of the most familiar expressions of pack drive is when we take a walk with our dog. We call it a *Purposeful Walk*. We do this every day, and yet for so many owners it is not simply a chore but an ordeal. The dog is out in front, pulling on the leash, with the frustrated owner following behind, barking, "Heel, heel!" What would the walk be like if the dog was walking politely next to the owner at the owner's pace, even without a command? How would that affect both of their lives? We will be expanding on this concept throughout the book and demonstrating how you will be able to achieve this easily with your dog. Being social creatures, dogs desire to be with us. The relationship is fulfilling for both dogs and humans alike. The fact is that the more the pack drive can be drawn out of a dog, the happier both dog and human will be.

Which brings us to how all of this relates to a training approach that uses an e-collar as one of the primary tools in its methodology. A dog's instinctive drives are what it brings to the training process. A key advantage to contemporary e-collars is that they can be used in extremely subtle ways that take into account the specific needs and strengths of the individual dog with whom you happen to be working. Dogs, like people, have different touch sensitivities, and being able to adapt the stimulation level of the e-collar to the personality of each dog makes training with an e-collar far less stressful than more traditional forms of training and, we believe, more successful. We will be explaining this in detail throughout the book, but suffice to say that our approach uses the e-collar primarily as a communicator through which the dog is able to learn and respond with clear understanding and appropriate motivation. Only with that foundation in place is it then used to interrupt unwanted behavior.

The right tools make the job easier for both you and your dog. This dog is modeling her 6-foot leather leash and e-collar.

CHAPTER 5

What You'll Need to Train Your Dog

At least twice a month, clients come to the monks' or Marc's dog training center with an e-collar they have already purchased, most often online. A quick Amazon search for the term "e-collar" returns over 1,000 results. And sadly, a search for "dog shock collars" returns over 5,000. Virtually all of the clients who come with their own e-collar mention they worry because they don't know how to use it properly. We understand that figuring out appropriate ways to use an e-collar by yourself is difficult, but even before that challenge, figuring out which collar to buy has stymied even professional trainers. While we can—and will—recommend some good-quality e-collars and point you to the features we think are most important (and those that are non-negotiable), there are hundreds of others that we would not recommend in all good conscience. That's because not all e-collars are created equal. The field is crowded and confusing, especially to those who have not spent years evaluating equipment and developing mild methods.

In this chapter we discuss what you should look for in an e-collar so that you can follow the lesson plan in this book and conduct your training in the gentle and compassionate way we have designed for you and your dog. We will also lay out for you a few other pieces of equipment you will find useful in training your dog. To help simplify the list, let's first break it down into categories.

Training Collars: We do not attach a leash to an e-collar. Rather, we attach the leash to a nonelectronic collar we will call a training collar in this book. There are several types of training collars, and we will discuss all of them so you can choose the right one for your dog's specific temperament.

Leashes: Your direct connection to your dog is through a leash that attaches to the training collar. Selecting the right type of leash for your dog will have a lot of impact on whether you can comfortably train your dog . . . or whether you will end up with sore hands!

E-Collars: With our method, the e-collar is used primarily as an attention-getter and rarely, if ever, as a punisher. That means we need to use an e-collar which is not only reliable but is also capable of delivering a subtle sensation with precise timing.

Long Lines: As the dog becomes more and more trained, you'll want to let him get farther away from you to enjoy running, playing, and just being a dog. Our long-range goal is to establish off-leash reliability, which means your dog listens to you even if he is far from you and distracted. Long leashes, called long lines, will help us achieve that goal. Eventually we will phase them out when we no longer need them.

Treats: A quick, tasty reward can help emphasize a moment when your dog has done the right thing. Given correctly and with the right timing, a treat will not only motivate your dog but also help him remember what behaviors you're willing to reward.

There are infinite variations for each of the five tools listed above. The advantage of having so many options is that you'll certainly be able to find tools that suit your training needs. The difficulty is that, without the right information, you can easily get lost among all the choices. What you want is the tool best able to help *your* dog most easily respond to the training process. It's funny, but the impulse is to look at the tools and pick the ones that you imagine you would want on you if you were a dog. Based on our decades of experience training, however, we've learned that dogs have their own unique way of seeing the world. They like structure and order, and that's what you'll provide with our training methods and with the collars, leashes, and treats we'll help you choose.

Selecting a training collar suitable for your dog's temperament makes training easier for you both

So let's take a close look at each of the five tools you'll need and explain how to decide which are best for your dog. No one knows your dog better than you, so we trust you to make these equipment decisions with your dog's best interests in mind, based on the information we give you.

Selecting a Training Collar

The training collar is not electronic. It is the collar to which you will attach your leash; it allows you to get your dog's attention when she is distracted. We never attach the leash to an e-collar because it is not designed to accommodate any pressure the dog may place on the collar by pulling. There are many training collar options for you to consider, and we will cover what we believe to be the most helpful ones here. The choice you make is important because it will have a great deal of impact on whether your dog learns quickly and without worrying. The right collar, when used with the techniques we will teach you, quickly helps your dog focus on you rather than on distractions. That's because your dog is likely to exert pressure against the collar, pressure that he will quickly learn how to remove. The wrong choice can inadvertently cause your dog discomfort because some dogs are more sensitive than others to even a slightly more corrective-feeling collar. So we will present the options here in order from the least corrective to the most. That being said, using the lightest corrective collar on a dog who needs more is not doing the dog any favors. That's because some dogs will nearly choke themselves pulling on a simple flat buckle collar, and yet they will quickly calm down and focus on what you are asking if you use a collar that allows you to mildly correct and guide them.

We have learned more than one surprising thing in our dog training careers, and one of the biggest revelations was how gently an artful trainer can work, even with corrective collars. So what is the best way to make a choice? We will list the collar types along with a description of how they work and what personality of dog they may best suit. Furthermore, we will list them in order from what typically works best for the mildest-mannered dog all the way up through the wild child personality type. We understand that you are likely new to dog training. Maybe this is your first time and you're finding this choice more daunting even than selecting an e-collar. So here is our suggestion to help you through this process in the easiest way possible for both you and your dog. If you are uncertain, it is always acceptable to start with the first type of collar on the list, use it for a few lessons or even a few days, and then evaluate your dog's reaction and progress. Then you can determine if you want to change to a different collar type farther down on the list. Conversely, at any point you may decide to change the collar, going in the opposite direction.

As you proceed, we believe it will become clear whether you have made the right choice, based on a combination of factors that include your dog's ultimate willingness to complete the lesson combined with minimal or no discomfort. We have certainly met dogs who, after a few days on a lightly corrective training collar, stopped worrying altogether about it and who ultimately performed better and easier with a more corrective collar. We have also trained dogs who have gone the other way with their collar needs.

At the end of the day, the training collar is not intended to scare your dog into doing the right behavior. It is intended to help you make the right behavior slightly more physically rewarding than doing the wrong thing, while simultaneously making the correct behavior far more emotionally rewarding. If anything, be willing to err on the side of caution. But also be willing to make adjustments up or down a level if you perceive the need. All of the following collars come in a variety of sizes.

Here are the collar varieties we recommend for various dog temperaments, most of which are shown on pages 76–77. They are listed in order of disposition, from very mild-mannered to wilder dogs.

Flat buckle collar. Made from nylon with a clip or from leather with a buckle. While this is the least corrective collar and many people already have one for their dog, we find that only extremely mild-mannered dogs will train well on this type of equipment when you apply the techniques and lessons we will give you. It does have the advantage of being friendly looking, but the average dog will pull the leash so hard when on this type of collar that you frequently hear the dog coughing and choking. This is not good for the dog's trachea. It can even be dangerous for brachiocephalic dogs—those with short muzzles or pushed-in faces, such as bulldogs. However, if your dog already walks fairly well on this type of collar without extreme leash pulling, you may well be able to use a flat buckle collar. In such cases its main disadvantage is a dog's ability to back out of it. This kind of collar can slip right over

1 Flat buckle collar

2 Martingale collar

3 Starmark collar

5 **Prong collar**

6 **Back-up collar**

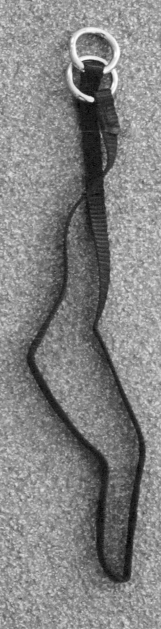

his head. So if you decide to use a flat buckle collar, we think it is extra important for you to use a backup collar.

Martingale collar. Slightly more corrective than a flat buckle collar, this type of collar is still quite mild. A martingale collar might be a good starting point for dogs who pull but who are not dedicated lungers who nearly take you off your feet. The collar is composed of two loops, the larger of which is usually nylon, and passed over the head of the dog, onto the neck. The leash is attached to a ring on the smaller loop. When the dog pulls on the leash, the smaller loop tightens and this, in turn, tightens the collar on the dog. We favor martingale collars which have that second loop made out of chain rather than nylon. The chain loop is where you attach the leash. The entire collar will feel loose to the dog, but if he pulls and you need to lightly pop the leash with a quick tug, the chain will make a small zinging noise audible to the dog. It won't scare him, but excitable yet mild-mannered dogs quickly learn to walk without pulling, as you will teach in the first few lessons.

This Yorkie is wearing a Starmark collar (size small)

Starmark collar. This unique collar is designed and manufactured by a company that also runs a school for dog trainers. It is a martingale-type collar with some important differences. The larger loop that goes around the neck is composed of plastic prongs. The smaller loop is made out of nylon cord. A quick attach/quick release clip allows you to put this collar directly onto the dog's neck without passing it over his head. That's important because you don't want to pass prongs over the dog's eyes. Although the prongs feel relatively pointy to us, we have noticed that very few dogs find them ouchy.

This is a good collar choice for dogs who often pull hard, assuming they don't nearly outweigh you. The Starmark collar comes in two sizes for large and small dogs. It is adjustable by adding or removing links, but it is important that the collar fit snugly on the dog's neck. In the rare event that a dog acts overly sensitive to the touch of the prongs, this collar can temporarily be flipped inside out so that only the smooth

Some dogs respond well to a prong collar with rubber tips

side touches the dog. This collar, therefore, is a good option for a large range of dogs. You'll probably need to order online, because it is not commonly found in stores.

Prong collar with rubber tips. Theoretically this collar is similar to the Starmark collar in that it uses a loop of prongs with a second martingale loop. However, in this case, the prongs are made of metal, also intended to be put on around the neck rather than passing over the eyes. These come in various sizes and can be found more easily online than in stores. The collar should fit snugly, but not uncomfortably, around the dog's neck. Small rubber tips cover the ends of the prongs. This kind of collar offers slightly more control for the moderate leash puller who is not very sensitive. The advantage is that the tips prevent metal from touching the dog. However, the prongs under the rubber are often sharp. Do not remove the rubber tips, and immediately replace any that fall off with use.

Prong collar. Admittedly this is a controversial collar because it features metal prongs and a martingale loop made out of chain. The brand we personally use and recommend is made in Germany by a company called Herm Sprenger. When it is used *artfully*, this collar stops the pulling and converts it to more focused behavior quickly and without drama. The trick is to introduce and use it in a very specific manner, which we will relay in detail in the first few lessons of the training plan. The collar comes in multiple sizes, although we recommend avoiding the largest size (4.0 mm) unless your dog weighs over 125 pounds. It should fit snugly around the dog's neck. One of the important benefits of this brand of prong collar is that the tips of the prongs that touch the dog are smooth and rounded. They are not sharp, and used as intended they will not scratch your dog. This collar is appropriate for moderate to extreme pullers from dogs weighing 15 pounds and up. If your dog proves too sensitive, you can quickly reduce sensitivity by connecting the leash to both the intended leash connector ring and to the separator ring on the martingale loop. This will prevent the martingale loop from tightening. Even sensitive but extreme pullers usually get used to this collar quickly when connected to both rings. Eventually most owners will be able to go back to connecting only to the leash connector ring.

CAUTION: We recommend you do not hang multiple dog tags on your training collar. They tend to jangle together and make a distracting noise. If you want to use a tag, use only your dog's ID tag. Do not leave a training collar on an unattended or unobserved dog, particularly not collar types 2 through 6. That's because those collars have a greater tendency to get caught on objects in the environment. Never allow your dog to play with another dog while wearing a training collar, because it can easily get tangled in the other dog's collar.

ALWAYS USE A BACK-UP COLLAR

This is an extra-long nylon slip collar that is attached to the leash and worn *in addition* to any training collar. It is used as a safety measure in case a training collar breaks. Also it will not slip over your dog's head in the event he tries to back out of it. It prevents your dog from getting loose in the event of equipment failure. Although we will not mention it in the lessons, we recommend you always use a backup collar regardless of what training collar you choose.

Selecting a Leash

Leashes come in many lengths and are made from a wide variety of materials. First, for the purposes of our training program, we recommend that you do not use a retractable leash, because our lesson plan is based on the use of a traditional 6-foot leash. Avoid rope leashes or other bulky and stretchy materials. The best leash for

1

6-foot leather leash

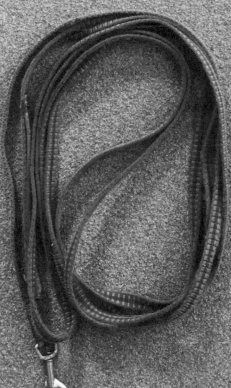

2

15-foot long line

3

20-foot parachute cord

training is made of leather and, depending on the size of your dog, is ½ inch to ⅝ inch wide. There are other widths for very small and very large dogs, so try them to find the best feel. Leather leashes are stiff at first, but they break in beautifully over time and will feel more comfortable in the hand than any other material. You may also choose a 6-foot nylon leash, but avoid those with two handles and material that is either very thin or very thick. The thin ones will burn your hand if your dog pulls hard, and the really thick ones are very difficult to gather together in your hand per the lesson instructions. Do not hang a poop bag dispenser or anything else on your training leash.

YOU'LL ALSO WANT A LONG LINE

A long line is nothing more than a long leash. We recommend a 15-foot-long cotton web or nylon long line. These are available at some pet stores and are easily found online. If you have a very fast dog who you will be training in open fields, you may want to have two 15-foot long lines that you can clip together, doubling your reach. You can shorten it by unclipping one as your dog becomes more reliable. You might want to wear gardening gloves when first using a long line, because it might give you rope burn if it's yanked quickly through your hands. In the final proofing stages of the recall, you may choose to use a parachute cord (easily available at large hardware stores) since it is so lightweight that it will effectively simulate off-leash situations but still give you the possibility of gently reinforcing the recall should your dog begin testing you.

Selecting an E-Collar

This will likely be the most important decision you'll make. And if you're not careful, it can also be the costliest in terms of money and—more importantly—comfort for your dog. We understand a natural tendency to shop for the best deal, especially when prices range from $40 to $400. But think about anything you buy that has such an extreme range in price. There's a world of difference in quality between a pair of cheap headphones and the more expensive ones. E-collars are the same way. They may look physically similar and their feature lists may overlap in some areas, and yet the ease of use and sensations felt by the dog vary enormously.

Further complicating matters is the fact that dogs come in many different sizes, with different length fur. Not only do dogs differ in physique and temperament, but the way an individual dog *actually feels the collar* will vary from one dog to the next. Remember, we most often use the e-collar as an attention-getter, not a punishment. Therefore, we always want to use an e-collar (and a level on that e-collar) that the dog can perceive at any given moment but which does not disturb him.

In our own dog training practices, we have often seen a curious phenomenon. One would expect that a big, muscular pit bull would generally require a stronger e-collar level than a much smaller labradoodle. But very often, and for reasons unknown, the 70-pound pit bull feels and responds to a lower level than a 30-pound labradoodle. You cannot look at

With our method, the right e-collar can be used as an easy attention-getter

a breed, or even an individual dog, and guess what he will feel based on how big or small he is or based on how muscular or fluffy he looks. The solution is to select an e-collar that is capable of great subtlety in the event it turns out your dog needs that. Most dogs will respond to sensations from the e-collar that humans barely feel, if and only if we use these subtle sensations as part of a training program designed to teach a dog that these tiny little signals are both important and understandable cues that have meaning.

All these factors can make it challenging for a novice to sort through the options to select the best unit for his or her dog. To make this job easier, we will tell you here which brands and models we favor as well as why. We'll also tell you about the features we find most useful so that you can independently evaluate e-collars to choose what will work best for you and your dog. You don't necessarily need to use any specific make or model. However, to train your dog with the sort of gentleness and clarity that we seek, you will definitely need an e-collar that can perform similarly to the ones we will reference here.

HOW MUCH SHOULD YOU SPEND?

In our experience, you should plan on spending close to $200 on an e-collar. Although that may sound like a lot of money, it is well worth it to help your dog feel comfortable during training and to be safer as a direct result of training. Plus it is certainly cheaper than repairing chewed furniture or damaged household goods. These are the features you're looking for in a good e-collar:

- The e-collar stimulation feels smooth and has a *minimum* of 15 levels, giving you plenty of options. Sensitive dogs may benefit from even more levels, thus more choices between low and high.

- There are separate buttons for "constant" and "momentary" electronic stimulation.

- The e-collar has lithium ion batteries that recharge in just a few hours.

- The batteries charge inside the unit; you simply connect to a charger.

- The e-collar has long-lasting batteries that only need charging once or twice a week with normal use.

- Both the e-collar and its remote control are water resistant.

- Range is at least 400 yards for small dogs, double that for medium to large dogs.

Take note of the manufacturer's warranty. Some companies offer very long warranties on parts in the event of a manufacturing defect. Many also offer 1 or 2 years' full warranty on parts and labor. Eventually all batteries fail. Check that the company you choose makes replacement battery packs available. Usually these can be installed by the owner, requiring only a screwdriver. Quality e-collars feature batteries that last at least 2 years.

Cheaper collars tend not to have any of these features. We have not tested *all* of the units in the $40 to $150 range, but we have certainly seen our share. They are often brought to us by clients who have already purchased them and couldn't figure out how to use them without upsetting their dogs and, therefore, themselves.

WHAT ARE THE KEY FEATURES OF GOOD E-COLLARS?

Ideally we want two buttons for constant and momentary electronic stimulation, each of which will be helpful for specific situations. The terminology may vary from manufacturer to manufacturer for these buttons, but what they actually do is this: the constant button will deliver an electronic stimulation for as long as you push the button. This feature is important to us and our method, given that we'll mostly be using the collar set to such low levels that it may take a brief moment for the dog to even realize that he felt anything. Some e-collar makers build a safety control feature into their e-collars which overrides and stops the stimulation if the constant button is pushed for more than 10 seconds. We think this is a good feature, but we can't think of a single time we have ever pushed that button for even close to 10 seconds. Usually we just give it a quick tap. Nonetheless, the 10-second override is a good idea, but we don't want to rely solely on that as our entire defense against accidentally overstimulating the dog. We'll go into other safety features in a moment.

The momentary button delivers a short, premeasured tick of stimulation, even if you hold the button down for a long time. We estimate that the duration of a momentary stimulation is one-tenth of a second. This is a handy feature because it allows us to give a quick and easy reminder to the dog if we need attention when he is only slightly distracted. Sometimes we'll also use it as a teaching device. As an example, in the lesson plans we'll use a light momentary tap as one of the cues associated with the *sit* command. Think of it as a single tap on the shoulder from a friend who wants your attention to tell you something. Tap, in our lexicon, means pushing either the constant or momentary button, usually quite quickly. Multiple cues, including that tick of momentary, slight upward leash pressure and a treat,

We strive for a loose leash and focus during our training

make it easy for the dog to understand what you're asking him to do. Over time we reduce the cues one by one until the dog will sit on a verbal command when you ask. We'll get into much more detail in the lesson plans, but momentary is a good feature to have. Although you can tap the constant button to emulate what momentary does, it is unlikely that any of us can push and release the constant button in a tenth of a second.

Some e-collars feature one button for that momentary tick of stimulation we mentioned and another for constant. Some also include a third button for either tone or vibration. Many dog owners also have outdoor underground fences. Their dogs wear a fence collar, which uses a similar tone to warn the dog that he is getting too close to the perimeter. Because fence collars tend to give the dog a decidedly unpleasant electronic correction if he ignores the warning tone, he quickly learns that tone is not to be ignored. So if you have an underground fence—and if your dog's fence collar has a warning tone feature—you may also find tone a good option in an e-collar. It won't be terribly useful in our training method, but it may be used to deter dogs who've been trained on electric fences from getting into the trash, for example. We don't consider a tone button important when selecting an e-collar.

Vibration, however, is another matter. We occasionally find this sort of stimulation useful as a deterrent—not so much during the initial stages of training, but once a dog truly understands that countertops and trash cans are not his personal buffet. The vibration button causes the little box to vibrate on the e-collar the dog wears. It feels very much like what happens when someone calls you on your mobile phone when it is set to vibration only. Because this sensation is highly tactile—something is actually moving on the dog's neck—the feeling, although benign, will cause a reaction in most dogs. Some dogs will stop what they are doing and look around to see what touched them. This gives us the opportunity to reacquire the dog's attention if he was lost in a sniff and not hearing our command. Other dogs may startle and be momentarily discomforted. With such dogs this gives us the opportunity to encourage him to come to us for reward and comfort, reinforcing the *come* command and teaching the dog to avoid forbidden or dangerous objects. A very few dogs find vibration so startling—they look like they are jumping out of their skin—that we avoid using it for anything other than teaching the dog to steer clear of danger.

We have trained numerous dogs with pica, the eating of inedible objects. More than a few of those had surgeries to remove things from their digestive tract. Those things have included towels, children's toys, disposable razor handles with blades, batteries . . . even golf balls! Eventually vibration can be part of the cure if the dog truly doesn't like the feeling. First we train the dog because training often improves this sort of behavior. But in the event the behavior persists, we'll give you more solutions in Appendix: Dog Behavior Problems. Suffice it to say we favor e-collars with a vibration feature. But the reason we do not primarily train with either tone or vibration is because, even though a percentage of dogs will consistently respond to them, the vast majority of dogs will eventually power through them to continue doing whatever their preferred behavior was versus what you are asking them to do. For example, you can use tone or vibration to teach some dogs to come when called even if they see a squirrel. However, a far greater number of dogs will reliably come with such a high distraction if they have learned with a variable level of electronic stimulation, which dogs seem not to tune out. Although we use it gently, electronic stimulation is more likely to be perceived in spite of the adrenaline rush dogs experience when they flip into prey drive. Therefore, although it may ultimately prove useful to have tone or vibration at our disposal, we want to use an e-collar that offers electrical stimulation.

OTHER FEATURES YOU MAY FIND IN AN E-COLLAR

Some of our recommended e-collars incorporate a light in the e-collar. The light can be turned on from the remote control. It allows you to see where the dog is at night if you have turned him loose in a dark area or yard. The light can be set to either solid or flashing. Some owners will have no use for this feature, but others find it a convenience or even beneficial for training. A client with a cocker spaniel named Gus comes to mind. Kathy reported that she had been able to train Gus to stop digging holes in her yard . . . by day. But Gus quickly figured out that he was free and clear to dig what Kathy called "the Mariana Trench" by night. We advised Kathy to turn on the e-collar light when she let Gus out in her fenced yard at night to potty. This allowed her to gently penalize digging, even at night, and soon the behavior disappeared altogether. As an aside, it turned out that Gus was quite a mouser, and mice had tunneled under the yard. Solving the mouse problem also helped Gus be successful. We always want to help the dog succeed.

Multidog collars feature one remote control that allows the owner to communicate with two or more e-collars. Different color buttons on the remote control correspond to different color straps on the dogs. Although we encourage you to train one dog at a time, many multiple dog owners who go hiking report that they feel safer knowing they can quickly get the attention of any of their dogs in an emergency. Some e-collar manufacturers allow you to start with a single dog collar, but later you can program one or more additional collars to operate from your original remote control. Other brands sell multiple dog collar sets already programmed for a set number of dogs. Just bear that in mind, in case you have multiple dogs you wish to train with e-collars.

One of our favorite e-collars has one other feature we particularly want to call out. That feature is called boost. By pushing a combination of buttons, you can instantly and temporarily increase your level without having to look for and touch the level adjustment knob. This is a time saver in the event of an emergency, when you won't have time to fumble with the remote. If the dog flips into prey drive, bolts for the street after a squirrel, and doesn't feel his normal level, pushing the boost buttons may be the trick you need. The amount of boost needed, if you need it at all, will be different for every dog and every situation. Therefore, the amount of boost is owner programmable.

SAFETY FEATURES ON E-COLLARS AND SAFETY SUGGESTIONS

Modern, well-made e-collars work by transmitting instructions via radio waves from the transmitter you hold in your hand to the e-collar receiver, a small box on the dog collar's strap. Old e-collars, and maybe even some cheap modern models, could be set off accidentally by other devices using radio waves, such as garage door openers or radio towers. They could even be set off by an e-collar remote control of the same brand that was within range and being used by a different owner. E-collars made by E-Collar Technologies, Dogtra, Garmin, and other quality brands use encoded radio signals with tens of thousands of combinations. This makes it statistically impossible for your dog's e-collar to stimulate him by anyone not holding his exact remote control unit. If you are buying an e-collar from a lesser-known brand, be sure to inquire how the unit will protect your dog from "false alarms."

Speaking of false alarms, one important safety suggestion we have for you is to safeguard the remote control carefully whenever your dog is wearing the collar. If you misplace it, or even put it down, someone from within or outside the household may pick it up and begin pushing buttons. Stick to manufacturers who provide you with a belt clip, wrist loop, or lanyard for the remote control. And if for any reason your dog is wearing the e-collar but you can't immediately locate the remote control, simply remove the e-collar from the dog. You can always put it back on when you locate the remote. This way you can be certain no one will find your remote control and begin to play with it.

As you handle your remote control, you may inadvertently change levels by knocking the intensity knob. Repeatedly putting the remote in a pocket and removing it also can accidentally change levels. So we suggest that you frequently

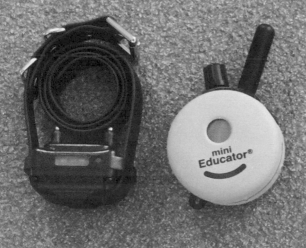
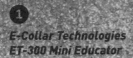

① E-Collar Technologies
ET-300 Mini Educator

② SportDog Brand 425X
Remote Trainer

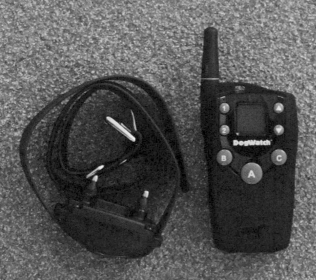

③ DogWatch
BigLeash S-15
Remote Trainer

4

**Dogtra 280C
Basic Electronic
Training Collar**

5

**Garmin Delta
Sport XC**

look at the level displayed on your remote to be sure it is where you want it. One of our most preferred collars has a safety feature you can use to digitally lock the level so it does not drift. We believe this is a very good feature to help you avoid causing discomfort to your dog via an unintentionally increased level. Whether or not you buy a collar that has this feature, be sure to regularly glance at the level display on the remote.

Finally, we suggest that you stay aware of how long your dog is wearing the collar. Because the collar is intended to be placed snugly on the dog's neck, it should be unbuckled, moved a few inches, and then rebuckled every 2 to 3 hours. We prefer the receiver to be slightly off to one side or the other, rather than being placed on the dog's windpipe. That means you can rotate from side to side. We also recommend that the e-collar be removed when you crate your dog, when you are not physically with your dog, and any time he needs neck rest. The dog should not have the e-collar on when he is sleeping at night. Although the brands we recommend are highly water resistant, we do suggest that if your dog gets wet, you remove the e-collar at your earliest convenience and dry your dog's neck to avoid irritation. See your e-collar owner's manual for more safety information.

A FEW SPECIFIC E-COLLAR BRANDS AND MODELS TO CONSIDER

Although we want to stress that the list we present here is not complete, this is a list of e-collars we have personally used and have confidence in. We understand that some of our preferences are purely personal. Most often, we train with and provide our clients with the Mini Educator by E-Collar Technologies, but we know highly competent professional trainers who are comfortable using any of these models. Because your needs and your preferences are based on many individual factors, please research carefully before making a final decision. For example, some of the remotes are smaller than others. That might be good for those with smaller hands, and less so for those with larger. Some have level numbers that are brighter or bigger than others, which might be important for those with poor reading vision. Some retailers stock multiple brands where you can examine and handle them all. Finally, think about contacting local dog trainers who train kindly with e-collars.

There are a growing number of them. In fact, both of us have personally trained many of them.

- **ET-300 Mini Educator from E-Collar Technologies.** Notable features include level lock, lights, choice of vibration or tone, owner-programmable quick level boost, half-mile range, programmable to go from single dog to two-dog unit.

- **ME-300 Micro Educator from E-Collar Technologies.** The collar receiver is 20 percent smaller and lighter than the Mini Educator and has 20 percent less electronic stimulation. The manufacturer rates it for dogs 5 pounds and up.

- **SportDog Brand 425X Remote Trainer.** Notable features include 21 levels of constant and momentary stimulation, as well as tone and vibration. Fits dogs 8 pounds and larger.

- **DogWatch BigLeash S-15.** Notable features include ergonomic remote control, half-mile range, 15 levels of momentary and constant stimulation, plus bright LED nightlights.

- **280C Basic Electronic Training Collar from Dogtra.** Notable features include an easy-to-hold remote control that fits most hands, easy-to-reach buttons, 127 levels of momentary and constant electronic stimulation, half-mile range, waterproof collar and remote.

- **iQ Mini from Dogtra.** Similar in features to the 280C, but with a smaller collar receiver and smaller remote. It also has unique conductive plastic points rather than metal.

- **Delta Sport XC from Garmin.** Notable features include 36 levels, ability to expand from one dog to three dogs, ¾-mile range, and a built-in bark-suppressing collar mode.

- **600 Yard Remote Trainer from PetSafe.** Notable features include 600-yard range, ability to expand from one to two dogs, and tone as well as vibration; has 15 levels of electronic stimulation.

Selecting Treats

The perfect treat is one that your dog *really* likes! Avoid crunchy treats because they take too long to eat and make crumbs that will distract your dog from the task. The best treats are about the size of a pencil eraser because the dog can gobble them in one gulp. In our training plan, treats are used in a very specific way and with precise timing to help dogs learn the behaviors you are requesting and remember which behaviors you are willing to reward. Avoid treats with chemical and artificial ingredients. Keep it healthy! In our dog psychology book, *Let Dogs Be Dogs*, we gave a recipe for homemade, single-ingredient liver treats. Dogs go wild for them. You can buy them freeze-dried and cut them small, or make your own. Pet stores have many other training treats to choose from, depending on your dog's preferences. We know that not all dogs are food motivated. If your dog just doesn't like any kind of treat, don't worry. You'll simply substitute warm praise. But for those picky dogs who don't like much else, we do find it handy to carry a plastic bag of cubed chicken breast for training rewards.

Miscellaneous Other Equipment

Chances are that you're coming to this book with some dog tools you've already tried, or you have heard of something you're considering. We thought it was worth mentioning a few of the items clients have asked us about during training sessions.

Harnesses. These come in many varieties. Some connect near the dog's shoulders, others in front of the chest. A few anti-pull designs squeeze the dog under the legs to make pulling uncomfortable. Others turn the dog sideways every time he tries to pull. Harnesses with no anti-pull feature tend to make the dog want to lower his center of gravity, dig in, and actually pull harder. Harnesses restrain the dog more than train him, so we do not use them in our method.

Head halters. Primarily designed to make walking on the leash easier, halters such as the Halti and Gentle Leader are designed to be worn on the dog's head, with a loop that fits over the dog's nose. This means that the dog's head will turn toward you if he tries to pull on the leash. Many dogs won't initially tolerate a halter and try to pull them off, but with training they can be quite useful. That said, we do not use them in the advanced portions of our lesson plan. That's because as time goes on we allow the dog to run ahead of us, and we are concerned the dog could be injured if he runs to the end of his leash or long line while

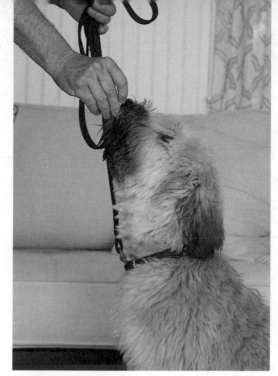

A small treat given at the exact right moment can help a dog learn more quickly

wearing a head halter. If you would like to explore these products, or if you already have one, we think they are best used when walking your dog by your side.

The Sidekick by K9 Lifeline. This unique leash combines multiple functions into one item. It can be used as a traditional slip lead with built-in collar. Due to its patented design, it can quickly convert to a head halter with built-in leash. This product also has a built-in safety clip which attaches to a backup collar. This leash/collar/head halter product can be useful in the event you have an extreme puller who proves overly sensitive to prong collars. You could use the manufacturer's instructions for the head halter function to teach the dog to stop pulling, and once that is accomplished you can proceed with our lesson plan, either using the transitional leash around the neck only or going back to one of the listed training collars with better results. This leash can be sourced online.

The e-collar is a communication tool that tells your dog to pay attention to you

CHAPTER 6

Let's Talk About Levels

You will be communicating with your dog using the e-collar, the leash (or long line), your voice, and maybe most important of all, your body language. This communication will teach the dog what you want him to do and help him actually want to do it with you. Remember: good training is not something you do *to* your dog. It is something you do *with* your dog. Moreover, e-collars do not train dogs. People do. An e-collar is merely a tool we use to communicate with the dog. We will use it primarily as an attention-getter.

We will provide the dog with simple, and we daresay fun, teachable moments. These moments will help your dog learn critical skills that every dog owner wants, such as to come when called and not to overreact to nearby distractions, such as other dogs, bicycles, or joggers. As we begin the teaching process with the e-collar, we will push a button to catch the dog's attention just as we begin each component of an exercise. The button itself doesn't mean anything. The critical part is *what you do* at the precise moment you push the button delivering some level of sensation to the dog.

Think of it like this: you are walking in the company of a friend, content together, but you are daydreaming for a moment and not paying attention to him. He wants your focus, so he taps you on the shoulder. The message might be, "Hey, we need to go *this* way; let's turn here." Or it might be, "Can we stop a moment? I want to look at something." It could even be something critical like, "Stop! You nearly stepped in front of a moving car!"

The tap on your shoulder merely sends you a signal to pay attention and focus for a moment because information is coming from your companion. In the culture of human body language, we become aware of this attention-getting method early in life. Most of us are using it ourselves not long after diapers come off. Why? Because our parents used it with us quite early on. Humans have spoken language in common, so when we touch one another in the "tap on the shoulder" analogy, we intuitively understand this is a signal that more information is forthcoming, usually in the form of spoken words, sometimes accompanied by gestures.

Now let's replay the scenario of walking with a friend. But this time your cell phone rings, and when you go to silence it you realize it is your boss or your child's babysitter. You excuse yourself to your friend. "Sorry, I have to take this."

The conversation flows as you walk, and let's assume that, without realizing it, you find yourself deep in conversation. Your boss is excitedly telling you about a huge new project that could net you both a bonus. Or the babysitter sounds worried, asking you where you keep the first aid kit because your 7-year-old has just fallen off her bike and scraped her knee. The conversation has your full attention.

Your friend taps you on the shoulder because he wants to tell you something. You don't notice. Your friend taps you again, probably slightly harder. Maybe you don't notice or maybe part of you does, but you are distracted, so you mentally shrug it off. Your friend taps you *again*, not painfully, but more insistently. Finally you look at him.

"We missed our turn," he whispers. "Just follow me and we'll go back," he adds, gesturing that you should follow but aware that you need to continue your call.

The tap in our second scenario, the one when you were distracted, was harder, wasn't it? Why? Because your friend instinctively knows that a distracted person requires a slightly more insistent touch to break focus on something else and turn it to him so he could deliver that message. Mission accomplished: your friend gave you the information he needed to provide in that moment. Quite possibly, though, there is a secondary effect, which is that as you resume your cell phone conversation you remain more aware of your surroundings than before, and you keep an eye on your friend, reminded that you are not alone.

In a similar way, you will probably notice that as training progresses, your dog will begin to remember that he is not alone, that the walks you are taking are togetherness events. You will see him begin to give you this extra bit of attention more and more easily as time goes on.

As we train the dog, we'll use varying levels of sensation. The levels will change to match the needs of the moment. Your dog will feel and be willing to respond to a lower-level feeling when there are no distractions present. Conversely, it will take a somewhat higher-level sensation for him to feel anything when distracted. Because we want to start slow, low, and easy, we'll begin by teaching simple exercises in the lowest distraction environment possible. This will allow us to catch the dog's attention with a combination of a low-level e-collar tap matched with some of your own body language that will make it obvious to your dog what the tap means.

When we talk about levels, we're referring to the intensity of any sensation we deliver to the dog with the e-collar. Think of it as volume which can be adjusted up or down

Used artfully, the e-collar and body language help a dog calmly focus on the trainer

according to the needs of the moment. Unlike sound volume, e-collar stimulation levels are tactile rather than auditory. Your dog feels them rather than hearing them. Like volume, too little will either go undetected or be ignored by the dog, and too much will register as minor or major discomfort.

The collars we use and recommend are capable of such subtle and low electronic stimulation that we always want the owner to feel it on their own skin before working with the dog. Owners are universally surprised how gentle the feeling is. Most people need to feel it repeatedly before they are even sure the collar is working.

Shortly we will walk you through the process to test the collar on your own hand, but let's discuss a few more details first.

As described in Chapter 5, What You'll Need to Train Your Dog, the best e-collars offer both momentary and constant stimulation, most often with a separate button for each.

Momentary stimulation is exactly what it sounds like: a quick tap, about $1/10$ of a second in duration. It doesn't matter how long you hold the momentary button down. It will only give that superfast tick of electronic stimulation at whatever level you have set your collar. If you want to tap again, you have to hit the button more than once.

On the other hand, constant stimulation means that a rapid series of electronic pulses continue as long as you hold the button down (tap-tap-tap-tap). Because we will be using the lowest possible levels your dog responds to, we will rarely even hold the constant button down for a long time. We are more likely to tap the button. When we do that, rather than a single one-tenth of a second momentary pulse, the constant button is going to deliver something like a half-second tap, significantly longer than momentary but still quick.

Think of momentary as if someone has touched your shoulder with one single tap. Constant is more like when someone taps you several times on the shoulder in quick succession. Depending on the situation, with people and with dogs, one might be better than the other. We'll talk more about that as we discuss the training exercises.

Then there is the vibration option. This is exactly what your cell phone does when it is set to silent. The vibration level is variable on a few collars. With most it comes with a single preset level. Vibration is accomplished by a rapidly shaking battery within the housing of the collar when you push the designated button. Because the collar is fixed snugly on the dog, a sudden vibration sensation can be somewhat startling to some dogs. Other dogs merely find it a curious feeling. However, most dogs will momentarily stop what they are doing when they feel it. This is what may make vibration useful during training.

Vibration is useful for many dogs, but how we use it is going to vary from dog to dog. We will find an appropriate moment to test his reaction so we can determine how to use vibration with your dog. If he is very startled by vibration, then we would not want to use it often, lest we make your dog jumpy. But we can occasionally use it when we need a strong aversive. In such a case, it will be important to use this sensation in a way that is educational. We want the dog to learn from his experiences so he need not repeat anything he finds unpleasant very often.

We trained a border collie mix named Tippy. He intensely disliked the vibration sensation. We know this because at some point in the training of a dog, we find an appropriate moment to test the vibration button, often when the dog is sniffing something he shouldn't. At some point Tippy inserted his nose in a garbage can and we tapped vibration. He nearly jumped out of his skin. He didn't go back to the garbage can, which was a good thing. But, as trainers, we understood that we should reserve that button for the rare moment when we wanted to apply an aversive.

Days later, Tippy caught a mouse in the training field. He proudly came when called and dutifully sat in front of us when asked. But he stubbornly held onto the mouse, even when told to *leave it*. We'll go over how to teach the *leave it* command in Lesson 15. Suffice to say that when Tippy ignored the *leave it* command even when accompanied with a tap of the constant button set a little higher, we shifted our grip on the e-collar remote and tapped the vibration button. With a startled leap, Tippy spat out the mouse and looked at it glumly.

Jump ahead another week and Tippy was nearing completion of his training program. Once again he somehow caught a mouse in the training field, and again he promptly came when called, sitting in front of us, holding his prize. *Leave it*, we said, not pushing any button. Upon command, Tippy quickly spat out that rodent, but unlike the last time, he still looked quite proud of himself. If you should find your dog reacting dramatically when you test vibration, reserve that button for moments when you really need to insist on avoidance.

On the other hand, your dog may not find the vibration feeling at all troubling. If that is the case, we can't use it as an aversive. However, we can use it as an attention-getter. Marc's German shepherd Sheena went deaf in her old age. Years before, Marc had trained her with the e-collar but had never found a good use for vibration. Sheena felt it, but she didn't much seem to care about it. When she went deaf, Marc quickly taught her to come when "called" by vibrating her collar and teaching Sheena to come find him for a pat and a treat.

Still, it has been our experience that most dogs will respond better to electronic stimulation than to vibration in most aspects of the training. We presume this is because the electronic feeling is actually more subtle than vibration, as well as being more easily variable in intensity.

We're here to make training fun, not drudgery. We think that using the e-collar allows you more freedom to actively practice rather than stick with rote drills. Because of that, and because we're embarking on something that is probably new to you, you may have a normal concern about whether you can do this. You may ask yourself, "What if I do it wrong? Will I hurt my dog?"

Here's our advice: follow the order of this book, especially the steps that relate directly to teaching the dog the sequential steps we will lay out for you. *Do not skip steps.* Some dogs grasp the foundation so quickly that owners are tempted to jump ahead in the training and move on. The owner becomes bored, worries that the dog will lose interest, or is still concerned about the idea of using an e-collar at all. Remember: we are *not* trying to hurt the dog. We do *not* want to hurt the dog. The steps are formulated to *ensure* that we don't hurt the dog. But if you skip steps and move too quickly, rather than keeping it interesting for your dog, you'll simply make it difficult for him to really *absorb* each step and each lesson. Eventually that will make it harder for him to apply what he has learned because he'll only have half-learned it. And that may cause you to do one of the following: turn up the collar needlessly; confuse your dog; or give up in frustration.

So don't skip steps or lessons, no matter how tempting it might be. You may already have realized that there's an appendix on problem behaviors at the end of this book. You may read it before you even begin training your dog, but start and finish the training process before applying this appendix with your dog. It won't be time to use those solutions until after you have completed the work in the prior chapters. There are two reasons for this.

First, you may be happily surprised to find that you don't have nearly as many problems to work on once you have trained your dog. Many dogs simply give up the problem behaviors that were troubling you when you first began. Both of us regularly witness the transformation in being able to walk politely on leash with a dog within the first several lessons. As your dog learns what we call a Purposeful Walk, the relationship develops and cooperation grows. At the same time, your dog's boredom and frustration will diminish. Many of the problem behaviors that probably drove you to buy this book may have disappeared or at least diminished in intensity as you and your dog come to understand one another better. That's because boredom and frustration are the root cause of many problematic dog behaviors. As you train your dog and spend quality time with him, the dog will be far less bored and frustrated.

Second, if you do still have problem behaviors to work on, by following the steps in all the preceding chapters, you will have given your dog a foundation of understanding to work with. He will understand "the language of the collar," (i.e., the meaning of the sensations he feels), allowing you to guide him toward the behavior you wish of him. Trust us when we say that a trained dog stops his shenanigans a lot easier and with gentler guidance than an untrained or partially trained dog.

We will talk about, and ultimately use, different levels for different situations. In this discussion we will mostly be referring to levels of the momentary and constant buttons. Just like shoes, one size does not fit all. What one dog literally cannot feel may be upsetting to another dog. Size and "toughness" of breed are not relevant here. A 70-pound pit bull may be more touch sensitive than a 10-pound Yorkie. In fact, we often find this to be the case.

In training the dog, we think of levels in two terms. The first is educational, light but detectable when there is no major distraction. Remember our example when your friend tapped your shoulder as you were daydreaming? That was the educational level. The second is what we call the reinforcement level. It is more insistent, more likely to register on a distracted mind. Our example for that occurred when you were involved in a compelling cell phone conversation but your friend needed to momentarily divert your attention.

The educational level is one that your dog can just barely feel at any given moment, but gets his attention. It is a sensation that just crosses the threshold of perception.

With our method, many dogs respond to sensations that humans can barely feel

Your dog can feel it, but barely. Because heavy distractions in the environment will push the threshold of perception up, we begin with a low distraction environment and activity when we seek to find a dog's educational level. The easiest way to identify this level is in doing the tap and turn exercise we describe in Lesson 4. We will flesh this out in much greater detail there, when we are using the e-collar for the first time.

The educational level will be different for every dog. And an individual dog's level will vary, according to what is going on around her at any given time. What a beagle will barely feel when she is indoors and calm may be very different from what she will barely detect when outside with her nose down, smelling where the rabbit has been. So we'll start with a low distraction environment and task.

The reinforcement level is a bit higher and therefore slightly more insistent than the educational level. Done correctly and at the right time, your dog won't find it disturbing. We certainly wouldn't call it painful. But if you consider carefully, you'll note that the reinforcement level was harder to ignore than the educational level. That's because the dog was more distracted and, therefore, less touch sensitive.

The interrupter level is higher still but used less frequently. It is reserved for situations when the dog is *highly* distracted and we wish to redirect her attention back to us. Because in our method we educate a dog in each exercise carefully using low levels, we build compliance and reliability by introducing distractions slowly and carefully. We go to interrupter levels only when the dog fully understands what we're asking but decides not to comply due to a high-level distraction. The level varies with each dog and is always the lowest that gets the dog to redirect her attention.

Years ago, Marc recalls a neighbor knocking on the door to tell him that a little brown dog was running loose near his house. Moments before, he had let a client's dog out into the fenced yard, and it found a previously undiscovered hole in the fence.

The dog had only recently arrived for her training program, which meant she didn't yet have a reliable come when called command. When Marc appeared she was quite happy to see him, but only so she could play her favorite game: keep-away. Marc knew he needed to get reasonably close to her so that he could get down on the ground and invite her into his lap. Thus began a merry game of chase. He ran a few steps every time she moved away from him and wasn't looking. Marc didn't want her to see him running after her because she would have just run faster.

It took a few moments, but finally the little dog turned around, to find Marc only a few feet away, sitting calmly on the ground, patting his thigh. The dog did the logical thing and jumped into his lap for some petting. Game over. Marc called it a draw. The dog was safe and sound. The fence would be repaired. Naturally Marc had been a bit excited and worried until he had her safely back in his arms. At the time, however, it was important for him to maintain at least an outward calm so as not to agitate the dog and cause her to really run away.

Dog safely crated for a rest, Marc sat down to take a breath, calm down, and think about fixing the fence. That's when he noticed that his leg felt funny. It didn't hurt. It just felt different than usual. So he looked down and realized he had a thin bead of dried blood running a few inches down his leg, originating from a scrape on his knee. It confused him for a moment, but as he assessed the minor damage, Marc remembered that during that not-so-fun game of keep-away he had fallen and must have scraped his knee. Yet he was so focused on safely retrieving the dog that he didn't even notice. Marc didn't detect the injury at all, not until he had calmed and his adrenaline level had gone down. In fact, he barely remembered falling at all.

When we are distracted or excited, our adrenaline level goes up. And as it does, our touch sensitivity goes down. This is a natural response that everyone understands, even if we don't usually have cause to think about it.

Both of us, the Monks of New Skete and Marc Goldberg, train dogs in our board-and-train programs. Owners book their dogs into school, and on the appointed day, come to either the monastery or Marc's Little Dog Farm. There, Brother Christopher or Marc will thoroughly discuss the training goals and tools with the dog's owner. Most importantly, we will want our clients to feel the e-collar on themselves before we ever use it to train the dog. That's because we want the owner to be giving not only consent but informed consent for the training. Plus, we have found that it really puts owners at ease once they have felt the e-collar.

Although most people are a bit uncertain beforehand, once they have felt it, we almost always get the same amazed comments: "That's it?" "You really think my dog will even be able to feel that?" When children are present, they almost always ask "Can I have a turn?" You don't have to do it, but this exercise is one most people appreciate, particularly if they're worried about the e-collar.

In the earlier discussion of equipment, we told you we prefer e-collars with many levels, and those often feature a rheostat level knob. Turn the knob and the level display climbs increment by tiny increment, usually from 1 to 100. Some collars have many fewer levels, say five or 10. Generally their level 1 is not quite as low as level 1 on our preferred collar, but it is likely that their top level is nearly the same as level 100 on our collar.

In the case of a collar that has 10 levels, rather than our 100, this simply means that every increase of one level is equivalent to at least an increase of 10 levels on our collar. And this means that, for many dogs, such collars are far more likely to cause discomfort at least some of the time.

Your perception is not necessarily going to be the same as your dog's. However, we hope you're using one of our recommended e-collars and that there is a wide range of levels available. We've found time and again that more levels are far better for the comfort of the average dog. It is worthwhile for us to have made that point repeatedly, because we don't want you to accidentally overwhelm your dog simply because your equipment has limited options.

Examine your e-collar and its owner's manual. Learn how to turn the collar and remote control on and off. Familiarize yourself with the various buttons on the remote, paying special attention to setting levels and which button is your constant and which is your momentary button. Note that terminology may differ a

Depending on the size of your hand, you may be able to hold leash and remote control in the same hand

bit according to the manufacturer. Some makers label as continuous what we have called constant. An alternate term for what we call momentary stimulation is "nick." This all depends on the brand, but the concepts are the same as we have outlined.

Turn on both the collar and remote. Select the lowest level, according to your unit's display screen. Find the constant button on the remote and set the remote in front of you. The collar will typically have two rounded metal contact points that are intended to touch the dog. Using your pointer and middle fingers *from the same hand,* touch the contact points firmly while using your thumb from that same hand to secure the collar receiver box. Don't grip with maximum finger strength. A solid grip is all that's needed.

Now give the constant button a quick tap. Did you feel a brief tingle or unusual sensation in your fingers or hand? If not, tap another couple of times to be sure. Then, if necessary, go to level 2 and repeat. Continue raising the level and giving a couple of taps until you can define a tingle or "funny" sensation in the fingers touching the contact points or even in a different finger on that same hand. Eventually, you will feel it. When testing the Mini Educator on our clients, very few feel it before level 8. Marc, who is quite sensitive, doesn't usually detect any sensation until level 9. Brother Christopher is less sensitive. He won't often feel level 9. In fact, he may not feel anything until level 13. By level 13 Marc will want to stop advancing the levels, yet Brother Christopher is able to advance through about level 25 without discomfort.

Different people describe the feeling differently. Some find it "tickly," and it may provoke a laugh. Others find it odd or mildly "weird." Almost no one finds it painful. Advance slowly through the levels until you are sure you have felt the stimulation.

People and dogs all feel the stimulation at different levels. The difference, of course, is that you know to expect the sensation, while the dog does not. That's why we use a feeling that will be just detectable to the dog. But for that barely detected feeling to be meaningful, we must find a way to explain to the dog what it means and why he should pay attention to such a small thing.

Eventually, you'll be able to enjoy an off-leash walk in a park and still have your dog's attention

Brother Christopher moves out swiftly with the dog at his left side on a Purposeful Walk

CHAPTER 7

The Purposeful Walk

What could be simpler than walking your dog? For owners of untrained dogs, the concept of an enjoyable stroll around the neighborhood or local park remains impossibly far out of reach. Many dogs pull, lunge, and bark so uncontrollably that even a simple walk around the block or a visit to the vet becomes a chore to dread. Most of our clients have a drawerful of discarded collars, harnesses, and leashes of various sorts because they have tried and failed to find a magic bullet. Yet a solution doesn't reside in any one piece of equipment. The only real and lasting solution is to actually train your dog so that she understands it is her job to walk calmly and attentively by your side. Given proper education, most dogs actually seem happy to do their job.

The keystone of our program is a deliberate and structured exercise we call the Purposeful Walk. During a Purposeful Walk, your dog walks at your side with her head, neck, or shoulder (depending on your and her preference) close to your left leg. As Pack Leader, *you* are in charge of determining the following critical factors even for your little pack of two:

- The pace or speed of the walk

- The direction we go

- Which distractions we ignore and which we engage with

The Monks of New Skete taking their dogs on an off-leash Purposeful Walk

Instead of avoiding regular walks with your dog, imagine you both moving forward at the quickest rate you find comfortable. The leash is bundled in your left hand. Your dog leaves a bit of slack in the leash so she'll feel comfortable as she keeps pace with you, remaining right by your side. You march proudly forward, shoulders back, chin up, with a bit of spring in your step. To a passerby you don't look as though you are wandering aimlessly. You and your dog appear to be walking *purposefully*, a duo on a mission. You both notice other people, some with lunging dogs 4 or 5 feet ahead of them, yet yours remains calm and attentive because she has a job to do. You smile, remembering your own struggles before the Purposeful Walk.

What does the Purposeful Walk fix? Why does it work? And why is it important for you to understand it on the philosophical level before we go into the nuts and bolts of how to teach it to your dog?

As we discussed in Chapter 4, dogs are social pack animals. Due to their genetics, they desire contact not only with other dogs but, critically, also with people. They have a natural inclination to follow a clear leader. This is why we believe the Purposeful Walk is a foundational exercise for anyone hoping to raise a kind, socialized dog who gets along well with people and other dogs.

This is a deceptively simple exercise to teach. Once the owner learns the basics and teaches it to the dog, the dog becomes more obedient, and most important of all, the dog will become *far* more open to learning the advanced skills we will teach, such as coming when called despite distractions. That's because both dog and owner will fall into more communion with one another and enjoy an easier, more profound relationship once they have mastered our Purposeful Walk. But what do we mean by "more profound relationship"? Think about a natural linking of the minds so that you and your dog seem to know what the other is thinking most of the time. You'll just *know* when he needs to blow off some steam, and you'll make time to give him that opportunity. He'll *understand* when you need him to be calm and collected so you can get some work done. He'll either settle himself into a down near you, or he'll go off and find an approved activity such as bringing a favored toy or bone to his bed.

The vast majority of our dog-training clients come to us with complaints about what they want from the dog. "I just want him to listen," they almost universally say. Ironically, the clients don't often realize that listening implies dialog. Dialog is a two-way street, a conversation in which both parties have something to express and each needs the other to not only listen but also to understand the message and needs of the other. Naturally, our species wishes to express ourselves verbally, which we find the fastest and most direct method of communication. Humans can transmit enormous amounts of information to one another very quickly using words to describe intellectual or intangible concepts such as time.

"I'll be home in 10 minutes" means something very specific and easy to understand when you say it to a partner or a child who is old enough to read a clock. But we cannot give information in this same way to a dog. If we try, we may very well confuse the dog. As you leave, if you address your dog directly, and excitedly or guiltily say, "Don't worry! I'll be back in 10 minutes!" your dog will hear a very different message from the one you intend. What he actually hears is excitement in your voice, which implies that you're about to take him for a walk or some other favorite and fun activity. Or, if you sound apologetic, you've set him up to understand that whatever action follows next is going to be a negative one. Either of those will have an effect on your dog you neither intended nor anticipated.

In the first case he'll get wound up with anticipation, and then the very next thing you do is walk out without him. That leaves the dog in a high-energy state of mind, and yet he's compelled to release that energy on his own. If you're lucky, he'll only pace and whine or bark for a while. In the worst-case scenario, he'll go find an activity to engage in on his own, such as surfing all your counters or raiding the trash, and chances are you won't like it. In the second scenario, where you are left feeling and sounding guilty, anxiety-prone dogs may bark or drool for extended periods and may even tear apart a couch in an effort to self-calm or divert themselves.

Samantha and Aaron were a busy power couple. Samantha ran the legal department for her company, and Aaron was completing his residency in emergency room medicine. Because they worked long hours, the couple hired dog walkers to come at least twice per day to walk Archie, their Australian cattle dog, and Clyde the beagle. Right before they left the condo, usually for many hours at a stretch, Samantha and Aaron performed their daily ritual. They played with the dogs for a minute or two, said emotional farewells, and gave them treats. Understandably, they did so out of a sense of guilt even though the dogs lived in a comfortable home and dog walkers were never more than a few hours away.

Every morning as they headed for the elevator, they could hear the dogs, whom they had riled up only moments before, scratching at the front door. The door sustained damage, but Samantha and Aaron put up with it until neighbors began to complain that the dogs had started howling and barking for hours at the front door. Their next move was to crate Archie and Clyde with dog beds and toys. While that stopped further damage to the door, neighbors told them the dogs barked more frantically than ever. Plus the dog walkers reported that they were finding the dogs in a state of near-hysteria every time they came. That's when they called us.

We had a lot of work to do with this pair of friendly but now slightly neurotic dogs. The first thing we did was begin teaching Purposeful Walking to Archie and Clyde. Although they had been on many walks with dog walkers (and only a few with their owners), neither dog had been taught to walk calmly and attentively on the leash. They were both small enough for the dog walkers to hold them back when they pulled. Consequently they were accustomed to yanking and lunging through every walk. Clyde wanted to stop and sniff everything, which the walkers had always permitted. And they could barely prevent Archie from eating everything in his path. At first the dogs tried all their usual misbehaviors with us. They also howled in our kennel when they should have been resting.

Within just a few days, we began to notice a difference in both dogs. They started to walk more deliberately as they began to understand the rules of the job we were laying out for them. Instead of barking at every bird and trying to investigate every blowing leaf, both Archie and Clyde were giving us periodic eye contact and walking by our side, thus lunging less every day. Within a week we were able to start working on come when called, and as a consequence we were able to dramatically increase the exercise level each dog was getting. This exercise, along with the structured day, was calming to the dogs, and each of them, slightly too chubby for optimal health, lost a little bit of much-needed weight. They seemed to recognize we were guiding them to a new deal, one in which Purposeful Walking and focused exercise replaced guilty, emotional farewells coupled with walks that had no rules.

Ultimately both dogs learned to do the job that we as their Pack Leaders taught them, and as they did so, both became far more patient during the inevitable rest times. Eventually we'd have to wake the dogs up from a snooze to go for a potty or to eat a meal. Our next step was to teach Samantha and Aaron how to step into our shoes to become Pack Leaders rather than apologists in their own home. We also suggested the couple wake up early to take the dogs for that first daily Purposeful Walk, then take the dogs out again for another shortly after arriving home. We also asked them to show the dog walkers how to do the Purposeful Walk for the sake of consistency. Everyone was happier, even the neighbors.

Purposeful Walking with you as Pack Leader is the first critical step because it teaches your dog not only to understand you but to follow your lead, literally.

And it teaches you how to communicate with your dog in a way that he can understand: calmly and quietly at first, with body language and action rather than words. When communicating with dogs, we always have a choice between show

Following our guidelines, you'll eventually transition your dog into off-leash training

and tell. All our human instincts—our hard wiring, if you will—shout to us that we should tell our dog what we want using words. And if the dog doesn't perform as desired, not only are we inclined to repeat our nonsensical (to the dog) vocalizations, but we are highly likely to intensify the tone and volume of these same sounds that the dog didn't understand in the first place. Think of all those funny American tourists in Paris for the first time, trying to order in English. When the waiter doesn't understand, they repeat the same order over again, only louder. St. Francis of Assisi reportedly had a very salient piece of wisdom for his friars that is pertinent here. He said, "Preach the Gospel at all times. When necessary, use words."

You will find it more effective to use your body to show your dog what you want rather than merely using words. But as the dog begins to piece together what you're asking for, you'll be very happy to see him begin to give it to you. That's when we'll help you start to add in a few words to your lessons, just now and again at first, to bring the human element back into the training. This will allow you to use *your* instinct to say words and will better prepare your dog to live in our human world, which admittedly runs more on words than on actions.

In the Purposeful Walk, the dog actually learns from you. It starts when she allows you to choose the *direction* of travel, the *pace* of the walk, and critically, which *distractions* she stops to react to and which she ignores. Once we teach you to master this exercise, you'll enjoy walks on leash during which your dog doesn't pull or become reactive to the wrong things. Moreover, you'll be setting the stage for enjoyable hikes with your dog *off leash* where you don't have to worry about losing him. Stated simply, this kind of walk brings you and your dog into alignment so you both get what you need from the relationship. Remember, you and your dog together are a pack. And as the monks indicated in their 1978 book, *How to Be Your Dog's Best Friend*, you are the Pack Leader, responsible for making key decisions for your dog to ensure her well-being and safety. Taught correctly, your dog will willingly give you the leadership role.

Part of "well-being" includes the physical and mental energy release that all dogs need. Depending on age, breed, and personality, some dogs require more mental and physical stimulation, some less. But they all need organized activity—in which you as Pack Leader participate—in a profound and critical way. Many owners make the mistake of turning their dog loose in a fenced yard "to get some exercise and fresh air" as the dog's only opportunity for physical and psychological stimulation. No walks. No drives in the car. No structured games of fetch. That is very much like dropping a lone child off at a playground with no one to interact with. Constantly left alone in a yard, your dog will certainly get air, but that's about all. He'll quickly become bored and seek out for himself the focused and positive mental stimulation you should have provided.

If left outside alone for too many hours, day after day, otherwise friendly dogs may become reactive at the neighbors or their dogs, charging the fence line and sounding ferocious. If a dog practices this behavior often enough, it can become so ingrained that he may actually scare or hurt a neighbor or another dog if that fence should break or the gate is accidentally left open one day. So many of our clients report that their dogs dig holes in the garden, tear up landscape, eat mulch, run the fence line while constantly barking, and on it goes. Think about it for a moment. Exactly what else would you have the dog do? Jumping jacks? Crossword puzzles? Jogging?

A dog left alone in a yard has nothing to do other than build up an excess of two things: boredom and frustration. We understand that everyone, including dogs, needs to be tolerant of downtime now and again. They should, and can, learn to control their impulses. That's why dogs can indeed be trained not to grab and chew everything they can reach. Still, so much of what many people want out of their dogs is a long list of "don'ts." Don't pull on the leash, don't lunge at people or dogs on the walk, don't run away, don't chew the house and my belongings, don't bark excessively, don't jump on me and our guests, don't beg for food at the table, don't dig up the yard, don't eat off the counters, don't get into the garbage, don't scratch the doors, don't dig up the carpet, don't lick items in the dishwasher . . . the list is endless! We know your dog can and should learn all those don'ts and probably a few more that we forgot to mention. Don't worry, we're going to help you solve all those problems we have just listed. But understand some of those behaviors are driven by curiosity and intelligence, others by an excess of mental and physical energy.

Unreleased mental and physical energy cause frustration and boredom. We cannot say more emphatically that a bored and frustrated dog is going to act out in ways that range from subtle to outrageous. Some dogs may just constantly lick themselves, causing a bare spot on their fur, while others will eat the house. We cannot forget a call from a beagle owner who used to lock his dog in the laundry room time after time when he left for a long day's work. Because the dog pulled hard on the leash and because the owner was often tired after a 9- or 10-hour day with a commute, this poor beagle rarely went for the sort of walks or adventures that the beagle's nose and energy level demand. One day the owner came home and was shocked to see that his dog had eaten a beagle-sized hole through the drywall inside his laundry room, pulled out the insulation between the studs, and then ate through a second layer of drywall separating the laundry room from the living room. When this owner came home, he found his dog, happy as could be, in the process of gutting the couch, foam and upholstery dotted all over the floor. Boredom and frustration are a terrible combination for any dog. Lacking training and a Pack Leader to provide for his needs, most dogs will solve these problems by inventing their own activities. And we can assure you of this: left to his own devices, your dog will almost certainly choose destructive or even dangerous activities.

Of course, we know that beagle owner loved his dog or he wouldn't have called us. In fact, he felt guilty about locking up the dog so much. But naturally what he asked was how to make that home demolition stop. Yet here's the thing: a dog who is not trained, a dog who does not understand how to patiently trust that his needs will be met, is a dog who *cannot* stop the naughtiness. In fact, if you stamp out one frustration-relieving behavior, another is likely to appear in its place. Although they may have a useful role, a series of quick fixes like bark collars, anti-chew spray, and scolding merely means you will be playing Whack-a-Mole with bad behavior. To truly stop unwanted behaviors, we must go to the source of the problem and relieve it for your dog. With our method, the Purposeful Walk at the center, we can give your dog understanding that, as Pack Leader, you will make key decisions for the team; your dog will learn to have more patience and trust that you will provide enough structured mental and physical activity to keep him from going stir crazy, and that will actually allow him to be well behaved during your absences. Perhaps most importantly of all, you and your dog will engage in an activity that just plain feels good. It will feel good to both of you because you'll do it together. Your dog will enjoy it because it will be a good energy release, and although you'll be setting the rules and boundaries for the walk, he'll have ample opportunity to literally smell the roses and engage parts of his doggy brain that will satisfy the very nature of his species. And you'll be pleased because, possibly for the first time, you'll notice how the Purposeful Walk allows you to elicit the best from your dog. Even though you'll barely be speaking, you'll have the growing sense that your dog is finally listening to you. Although it sounds ethereal, we hope that you will begin to feel a sense of deep communion with your dog, as we so often do with our clients' dogs.

Have you ever had the experience of taking your dog for a half-hour walk, with the dog pulling, lunging toward squirrels, people, or other dogs and demanding to stop and sniff at every bush? You allow it because your dog seems to want it. Or maybe you spend most of the walk trying to control him. Yet when you get home, although *you're* tired from the exertion, your dog refuses to settle down. He might not have even calmed down enough during the walk to eliminate. Does it seem like you didn't accomplish anything on that walk, your dog is more riled up rather than calmer, and your arm is sore? This experience is so unpleasant that many people give up on walking the dog altogether. And so the cycle of excessive barking or destructive behavior continues or even intensifies.

It does not have to be this way. There is a flip side to this coin, and we want to help you achieve it.

Lest you think that well a well-trained dog is going to look robotic, it is important to reassure you that quite the opposite is true. While it is certain that a well-trained dog is often calmer, the dog still has all the same joy of life as before. But the frantic note that besets so many untrained dogs usually settles down. That's because through training and a more trusting relationship with her owner, the dog learns to calm herself. Moreover, most dogs can learn this through our method; using the signature exercise of the Purposeful Walk, they will learn to start making more good decisions, seemingly on their own. A good dog does what you tell him to do. You say *sit,* and he sits. You say *come,* and he comes. You say *off,* and he stops jumping. You say *leave it,* and he stops sniffing the counter.

What could be better than that? But there *is* better. Better even than a good dog is a great dog, and a great dog often does what you would want her to do without even asking. Good dogs grow into greatness, and we can help them achieve that. A great dog has learned to keep an eye on her Pack Leader and to organically "go along with the program," which is to say that if the Pack Leader is calmly occupied, the dog

A trained dog can calmly accompany you to an outdoor café

follows suit and settles somewhere nearby, ready for a change but not pestering for or demanding one.

Before we get into the nuts and bolts of exactly how to teach these concepts, we are asking you to imagine the radical shift in your relationship that will begin to unfold. We can also assure you that not only will your dog learn some basic concepts of how to please you, but you'll also pick up some critical lessons from your dog. Once you understand one another better, a new set of possibilities opens up.

Do you live in an urban setting with crowded streets? What if your dog was able to pass other dogs on narrow sidewalks without drama? How much better would life be if he could see squirrels running along overhead wires without lunging or barking? Think about how much more time you could spend together if your dog could lie down next to your table at an outdoor café or coffee shop. Not only would you be able to use the city's dog parks, but your dog would be safer because you could more quickly call him away from any scuffle that might break out at the far end of the park. Rather than running over to see what is happening, when you call, your dog will come to you, away from the trouble.

Do you live in a suburb with wide sidewalks that people rarely use? Your dog will be able to walk nicely with you, even if you pass a yard with barking dogs on the other side of a fence. You'll have school yards and parks near you where you may be able to legally take off the leash or drop it and let it trail behind your dog as he sniffs the ground, rolls in leaves, or brings back a stick. Yet you can call him away from a rabbit or bird. You might even meet neighbors you otherwise wouldn't see. If you have children, you can bring the dog to baseball or soccer games and keep him on leash politely by your side.

And if you live in a rural area, you can hike with your dog on or off leash, depending on where you go. If the dog should scare up a deer, your heart will beat a little faster, but you'll be amazed when you can call him back and he comes to you, proud and happy from the brief chase but understanding his Pack Leader needed him to let the deer win this encounter. If you have horses, cows, chickens, or other livestock in the area, you'll rest a lot easier knowing your dog won't chase or bother other animals. Remember, in many parts of the country it is still legal for a livestock owner to shoot a trespassing dog who is worrying the animals. Yet country life holds so many good options for a dog who responds reliably to his owner.

We remember a miniature poodle who was flown to Marc's Chicago area boarding school program all the way from Palo Alto, California. Buddy's family raised heirloom breeds of chickens as a hobby. Buddy's chief form of entertainment was his mischievous habit of chasing the chickens until he caught one. Then he would proudly march around the yard, carrying an angry hen hanging halfway out of his little mouth. He had never actually killed a chicken, but all the fuss was putting the hens off laying, and the owners worried that Buddy was working his way up to actually mangling their pet chickens, either accidentally or on purpose.

We began teaching Buddy in an area devoid of chickens. It's always best to start training in an area that doesn't have major distractions close by. This allows the dog to begin the learning process while confronting lower-level distractions such as scents and the movement of far-off birds. Recall that in the Purposeful Walk we teach the dog we'll be moving together through open space, but that the Pack Leader will choose the direction we travel, the speed of travel we use to get there, and the distractions we ignore as well as those we investigate. Ultimately we needed Buddy to ignore chickens. But one step at a time.

Over the course of a week we took Buddy outside, first teaching, then practicing the Purposeful Walk. He learned to enjoy the time outside but to turn south when we had been walking north, even if he wanted to see the birds that had been in front of us. In time we were able to give the dog more latitude, meaning that if he wanted to investigate a particular area of the field we let him do that, making sure that he looked back at us periodically, checking in and making eye contact now and again. We introduced a long line so Buddy could move about more, but we also practiced calling him to come to us if he strayed too far, ensuring that he understood the *come* command from various distances, first nearby and eventually from as far away as 100 feet or more.

Before long he understood that when we went out for a Purposeful Walk on leash, he was to walk alongside without pulling. And when on a much longer leash, a 15- or 20-foot line we use to start teaching attention at a distance, Buddy could explore more, but he knew that he should remain aware of where his Pack Leader wanted to go and respond accordingly, regardless of what distraction might have called his attention. Eventually he could perform the same without any leash at all. Once the dog understands that the Pack Leader has the right to insist he avoid any particular distraction, we can begin to permit the dog to enjoy harmless diversions such as picking up a stick or sniffing a choice spot in the grass. The only rule is, *we* get to say when and for how long. All that went well and according to schedule. Buddy had learned that some forms of play and investigation were approved and permitted, but that others were off-limits and that we would let him know which were which at any given moment. By now, the training had become so incorporated into Buddy's behavior— keeping an eye out for any change of direction or a *come* command—that training this dog no longer felt like training at all, either to him or to us. Purposeful Walking had become a building block to an organic relationship in which each gave the other what was needed. Buddy learned to honor our leadership role, which enabled us to overrule any decision he might want to make. And in return for this sense of confidence that we could trust him off leash, we began to let Buddy stray a bit farther from me to enjoy sniffing and rolling in the grass now and again. We were happy with one another.

Finally it was time to include chickens among the distractions. Off we went to visit Chad and Stephanie, who kept a few chickens as pets. We could tell that Buddy immediately remembered his favorite job as chicken chaser because he got excited when he saw those hens. But before we got too close to the birds, we tapped the button on the remote control, sending a small signal to Buddy's e-collar, at the same time saying, "Let's go," then turned away from the chickens, guiding him with the leash. Because this sequence was the same as when he first learned the beginning of the Purposeful Walk, Buddy never pulled on the leash to strain toward them. Instead, he reluctantly broke his focus on the chickens and followed us away, whereupon we praised him and fed him a few really good treats.

The Purposeful Walk is a moving exercise made up of components that teach your dog to literally follow your lead, allowing you to make key decisions. Moreover, the exercise is fun for your dog. Therefore, it will motivate her to work with you and give you what you ask of her during training because she'll simultaneously be receiving so much of what she needs to be fulfilled.

This simple exercise establishes a foundation that carries over into every aspect of life in the real world with your dog. Often we hear from clients that they attended several classes in which treats were the primary focus of the method. Many of their dogs learned to perform a trick or a command when all of the following are true: the dog is on leash; the distraction level is low; the dog is hungry or food motivated; and a treat is shown to the dog even before the command. The problem with this form of training is that all four of those statements must be true in order for the dog to respond to the command.

The problem, of course, is that these are not real-world conditions. The time you will most definitely need your dog to come to you is when he least wants to because he's reacting to a strong distraction. We don't start with those distractions. We build up to them in a logical progression so as to educate your dog in a fair manner that he can both understand and, critically, *want to do for you*. We want buy-in from the dog rather than rote mechanical obedience.

Training will look a little different depending on whether you live in the country, suburbs, or city. But depending on the weather and your location, you can start it in your home and then progress to a sidewalk, the long hallways of a condominium building, or a yard or park.

To sum up, the Purposeful Walk is a simple exercise, but it has profound impact.

As people who are closely in touch with the heart, mind, and spirit of the dog, please trust us when we stress the following point because everything about your relationship with your dog depends on this:

While you are wishing that your dog would only listen to you, believe us when we tell you she is longing for the same from you.

A shift in dynamics lies ahead of you. Your dog will listen to you far more because you'll speak fewer words, but you'll clearly demonstrate what you're asking for with your actions. We all know that actions speak louder than words. This is doubly so when it comes to teaching dogs. And in the process of moving through space together—with you as Pack Leader determining where you're headed, how fast or slow you go there, which distractions you explore and which you ignore—your dog will find a deeper level of satisfaction with you than he previously understood to be possible.

Dogs love their owners, but they are happiest when educated to understand the rules

Nothing is more powerful than when you and your dog feel not only love for one another but also a deep and abiding sense of respect.

At its best, training is an art form in which both dog and owner get what they need from the experience

CHAPTER 8

When Training Becomes an Art

What makes our time-tested method unique is not only that we will incorporate an e-collar into the lessons but that we will use it so gently that you may sometimes wonder if your dog even feels it. But it will be a useful teaching tool and, ultimately, a sort of invisible leash to remind your dog to pay attention when it's important. When it's time, we'll talk you through how to introduce the e-collar to your dog in our unique and organic way, which varies from what limited information is available on the internet. One internet suggestion is to fully train the dog, then use the e-collar to reinforce commands, meaning to punish the dog if she does not immediately comply. Not only don't we do that, but we've designed our method to motivate dogs so even minor discomfort is hardly ever needed, if at all. Some trainers introduce the e-collar to the dog by pushing a button, giving electronic stimulation starting from a low level but increasing in intensity until the dog has a physical reaction. We've found that dogs often feel a sensation without finding it necessary to advertise that they felt it. And if the intensity has gone high enough to make the dog twitch, blink, or flick his ears, the level may have gone high enough to actually bother the dog.

Instead, at the appropriate time, we'll show you how to seamlessly blend the e-collar's introduction into Purposeful Walking. We'll assist you in finding a level that your dog can feel, and which helps teach the exercise, but is low enough that most dogs will not overtly react. You'll just notice that your dogs begin to add extra precision and focus to the exercise. Because the e-collar is introduced as a communication tool, not a punisher, and is added into a moving exercise the dog already understands, she will not have a negative view of the training or equipment.

In fact, we find most dogs act happy when we bring out the e-collar because they know it means we're going to go have an adventure, a learning experience, and some time in which we will truly focus on them.

Early on we'll start teaching the Purposeful Walk, which is what we call it when we walk with obvious *deliberate intention*. We start this exercise using a standard 6-foot leash. The Purposeful Walk is powerful because it is a moving exercise. After the dog learns it, staying close to you, relaxed and attentive on a 6-foot leash, we will expand the exercise by transitioning to a 15-foot leash, called a long line.

By modifying and expanding the Purposeful Walk from a short leash to a long one, we gradually teach the dog to pay attention when completely off leash in outdoor spaces and eventually when far from you. Ultimately this will allow you to walk off leash through a dog-friendly park or hike in the woods. It even teaches your dog to come when called because the exercise helps bring the dog into pack drive, the instinct to follow and collaborate with the leader. Dogs are physically and psychologically built to move through space, investigating what is of interest and ignoring what is designated as off-limits by the Pack Leader. The Purposeful Walk is *intentional*. To an onlooker it would seem the Pack Leader is intent upon getting somewhere important. Picture a businessperson walking briskly through a crowded city street, determined to get to an important meeting. This is what you will look like when, as Pack Leader, you are walking with your dog. The Pack Leader notices what is present in the environment but does not react to anything unimportant, and she expects her pack to do the same.

Think of African wild dogs, now endangered, distant cousins of our domesticated dogs. The pack follows its leader through their range for miles at a time in loose formation, often at a trot or quick walk. The dogs are lean, stringy, and hungry as they migrate through their world. Trotting through the grasslands, the pack will see many game animals, the same species they hunt and consume. Although they are almost always hungry, no dog in the pack lunges, vocalizes, or even stares at the gazelle or antelope, whether they are far off or relatively close.

The pack instinct present even in your modern dog is particularly strong in these wild dogs. And it is this instinct which ultimately keeps them safe and fed. The formation moves along efficiently and swiftly in pack drive, following the leader, eating up ground and distance for as long as necessary until the Pack Leader notices something that calls her attention. She, along with her mate and the rest of the pack, may well have trotted past hundreds of game animals. But prey animals have an uncanny sense of when predators are hunting versus when they are simply on the move. The prey may note their presence, but they are not overly alarmed or fleeing at the sight of the dogs.

Prey drive is natural to dogs, but pack drive is what keeps them calmly by our side

Eventually there will be a shift as subtle as it is sudden. The Pack Leader will have spotted what she has been looking for: an old, very young, sick, or limping prey animal. Some vulnerability in its aspect will have called her attention. Her body language immediately changes and is instantaneously noted by the rest of the pack. A switch has been flipped, and she has quickly changed from pack drive into hunt mode, also known as prey drive. Do her pack mates charge willy-nilly into the herd, trying to figure out which one she was looking at? Far from it. They observe her and her gaze. Noting what she has designated as worthy of focus, the pack will react with the prey drive we described in Chapter 4. Even then, there is no wanton charge. Each dog has a role to play in setting up the hunt, maneuvering himself relative to the prey and ultimately driving the animal into a trap which has been set for it by certain pack members who are hidden, waiting for it. Prior to that sudden focus and tension in the Pack Leader, all dogs merely marched along in pack drive, hungry but *obedient of their own free will.*

Thankfully our pets don't have to hunt for a living. Many of them wouldn't be able to do it very well anyway because domestication and breeding have tempered those instincts. But prey drive and what governs that—pack drive—remain on some level, and you are about to bring out your dog's pack drive in a way that will probably

Molly doesn't hunt for a living, but she appreciates time with her owner close to nature

surprise and please you both. The African wild dogs must learn many intricate lessons about their form of Purposeful Walking because it must frequently lead to a successful hunt. Our version will be far simpler and in fact starts with one very mundane yet critical task: for your dog to turn around and follow you when you change directions. You'll never teach your dog anything nearly as important as "turn around and follow me." That's because once your dog gives you the right to determine where you are going together, you'll have his attention and his focus, and that's more than half the battle when training dogs.

In our method, the Purposeful Walk—whether on a short leash, long leash, or off leash—replaces the more old-fashioned, traditional *heel* exercise. When a dog heels, she must act much like a soldier marching in formation. It is impressive to behold that level of precision, but it is not comfortable to sustain for long periods of time. Constantly nagging with repeated *heel* commands on a walk actually teaches the dog to ignore you. Purposeful Walk is an easy concept for your dog to learn and easy for you to use consistently under real-world conditions.

Some months ago our friend Ann brought her beloved Lab mix Molly to New Skete for one of our popular workshops. She was interested enough in e-collars to have purchased one earlier, but she still wasn't sure exactly how to use it for more than a correction. We quickly realized that Ann loves her dog and wanted to safely hike with her off leash in appropriate areas with legal trails. Molly, being of a hunting breed background, has plenty of prey drive, so Ann wanted to be sure Molly wouldn't take off and get lost during a hike. She had read the monks' books as well as the one they wrote with Marc, but Ann is curious and detail oriented by nature. She really did want to see for herself how our method works.

By Day 4 of our highly focused 5-day workshop, Ann felt that she and Molly had made enough progress with their lessons to go for an off-leash hike on the 500 mountainous acres of monastery property. Much of the land is hilly and heavily wooded. The trails twist and turn through the hills and around the trees. It's easy to lose sight of a dog in these conditions. Halfway up the trail Molly scared up a deer, much like what happened to Brother Christopher in Chapter 4. Molly took off after the deer. Ann instantly lost sight of her. Remembering their training, Ann called her dog, simultaneously tapping Molly's e-collar, using the constant button on the low level where it had been set. When she didn't hear the dog coming closer, she slowly raised the level, tapped, and called again. Within a moment, she heard Molly crashing through the underbrush, making her way back. Ann called out again to help Molly find her, but since Molly was close and on the way back, Ann made the good decision to not tap the dog again. Molly appeared seconds later, wagging happily and with that big doggy smile all dog owners love to see.

Whew! It would not have been a good thing to lose our friend's dog, but it all worked out well. We would simply urge you to follow all the steps in this book a bit more slowly since we're not working individually with you and your dog. The learning curve, therefore, will likely be a bit slower than it is at our workshops, but we assure you that you can do this, and hopefully you'll find it fun as well.

There Is an Art to Living with Your Dog

The training lessons we have devised for you and which follow are designed to quickly create an understanding between you and your dog. They will help your dog to happily learn a few important behaviors, which will make him safer and also allow you to enjoy one another's company more than ever before. But formal training lessons will only occupy a small portion of your day. As we move forward we will offer concrete suggestions on how to integrate lessons into daily life so that training becomes even more convenient. However, we think it's important for you to make a few key changes in your dog's routine while you are in the first 6 weeks of training. These changes are designed to help your dog really absorb the education you are giving him. We urge you to consider them part of the overall training plan.

In our last book, *Let Dogs Be Dogs*, we explained in great detail the ways in which a good Pack Leader *controls and provides resources* to her dog. Resources are the "stuff of life." They are the key elements that your dog needs and wants. If you need additional help in this area, have a look at that book as well as the monks' previous books, *How to Be Your Dog's Best Friend* and *The Art of Raising a Puppy*. We can absolutely assure you that the suggestions below will turbocharge your training, make your lessons more effective, and foster a better relationship with your dog. After all, dogs crave a good Pack Leader to follow. Here is a quick review of the most

A good Pack Leader provides all the resources a dog wants in return for good behavior

critical resources and how you should provide them. We find that most owners will need to institute at least a few changes during the dog's training. It will be worth it.

Food. No more free feeding. Don't simply leave a bowl of food out, refilling it when it gets low. This may be an acceptable way to feed cats, but in the dog world a good Pack Leader leads her pack to food. The Pack Leader is the provider. Feed twice per day. Much like the matriarch of the African wild dog pack demands that her pack follow her calmly until she selects the prey, you will ask your dog for a moment of calm before putting down the food bowl. It may help if you have your dog sit for a moment before giving him the bowl. If you are persistent, you will quickly find that your dog learns to give you a moment of calm in order to earn the meal. You should carry this forward through your dog's lifetime.

Treats. Who doesn't like to give their dog a treat and see the joy it brings? Treats can make a very powerful reward. For food-motivated dogs, a well-timed treat can be an incredibly valuable teaching aid. But if your dog gets a treat just because he went outside and came back in, just because he looked at you and barked, just because he fixated on the cookie jar itself, then your dog is training you rather than the other way around. This month, let's eliminate all treats except for those which directly correspond to those mentioned in the lesson plan. Don't worry, there will be plenty of opportunities to give your dog a treat. We're simply going to give you the optimal moments to offer them in order to help you accomplish your goals. Here's a pro trainer tip: use very small treats, no bigger than a pencil eraser. Your dog will eat the treat quickly so you can continue the lesson without turning it into a distraction that takes too long to eat.

Toys. Many of us shower our dogs with presents and toys. For the next 6 weeks, pick up all the toys and put them away in a closet or drawer. Before you feel bad about that, let us assure you that the idea is not to *deprive* your dog of toys and mental stimulation. Rather, the concept is that you can become the *provider* of these fun resources over and over again in the following manner. When you think your dog would enjoy playing with a toy, select one for her and ask for a sit or moment of calm.

In return, give your dog the toy and allow her to play. We would even encourage you to play *with* your dog, provided you don't merely rile her up. Toys and games are exciting. Simply interrupt the action every once in a while, ask for the sit, then release your dog to play again. If you think your dog is bored with the toy you selected, put that one away and give her a different one next time. For the ensuing few weeks, you'll be like Santa, giving presents out in return for a moment of nice behavior.

Space. Just like the matriarch or patriarch of a human family may determine who sits where at the dinner table, you should make occasional decisions for your dog about where she will rest her body. The easiest ways to make this point are to have your dog off the furniture and out of your bed for the next few weeks, at the very least while you are using them yourself. For some dogs this will be no change at all because they weren't allowed on furniture in the first place. If this affects you and your dog, however, don't worry. By the end of our training program you can restore the temporarily lost privileges. But we think you'll find them valued more than before because your dog will have regained them during the same period when he is working harder than ever to please you. If your dog is already crate trained, *crate him for a half hour right before and after a lesson.* This is the easiest way to help the lesson sink in. Otherwise, use whatever room works best for 30 minutes of quiet time right before and after a lesson. We know from experience that this will help your dog absorb the lesson better.

Emotion. We are called "dog lovers" for a reason. We don't just like our dogs. We adore them. A few decades ago, the family dog was considered a pet. Today, the vast majority of dog owners think of the dog as a family member. They are shown ever more physical affection by their owners, but ironically, as laws have changed, dogs are allowed in fewer and fewer public places. Owners who work longer hours come home and shower the dog with affection out of some sense of guilt about leaving her alone. Too often the emotions shared cause overexcitement or even frustration in the dog. You know what we mean if you come home, greeting your dog emotionally and enthusiastically. You share emotion in an excited human manner, the dog responds by jumping in an excited canine manner, and in turn you reprimand her. This will be hard, but for the next few weeks, dial back not the love itself but the excited physical touch and verbal emotion you give your dog. Instead, reserve your words and obvious displays of affection for *calm praise* when your dog does something correctly *during a training lesson*. Difficult though it may be at first, if you try this, you will be astounded to find your relationship growing more profound. That's because it will be based on mutual appreciation and understanding rather than an excess of excitement.

Training Deaf and Hearing-Impaired Dogs

Before we begin, we want to mention that the training program described here is not only well suited to the average family dog but it is especially appropriate for deaf dogs. We know the challenges normally associated with training hearing-impaired dogs because we are often asked by their owners if we can help train them. From our discussions with these owners we have learned that they have very few effective options to teach their dogs to come when called with a high degree of reliability. However, this skill is critical to the safety and well-being of all dogs. Following our directions, the vast majority of dog owners will notice their dogs beginning to look at them more and more. The dogs "check in" to see if anything is needed. And ultimately for deaf dogs, the e-collar vibration or tap merely informs the dog that he is to look around and find his owner. Because all of the commands herein include body language as well as a verbal command, deaf dogs will naturally and easily learn what you're asking them to do. Just accentuate the hand signals slightly.

As they become senior citizens, many dogs lose significant hearing. One of Marc's dogs, a German shepherd named Sheena, started going deaf at age nine. But she was still able to enjoy off-leash life at Marc's fenced Little Dog Farm because Sheena had been trained with our method and she easily learned to come back inside after a jaunt when Marc vibrated her collar. We trained a dog named Keller who was both deaf and blind from birth. Yet Keller had an amazing nose. She was able to map and navigate her surroundings by scent. This remarkable dog learned to come when called with a tap of vibration that caused her to begin scenting for us. Dogs are incredibly intelligent, and we believe the training plan here respects that intelligence and partners with it.

THE 6-WEEK PROGRAM FOR GENTLE TRAINING WITH THE E-COLLAR

We are going to guide you through a 6-week plan, at the end of which you will have a trained dog. To simplify the schedule, we'll give you a training chart to help you navigate which lessons to incorporate and when. The chart also will show you which exercises can be taught simultaneously. In only a month your dog will have good manners on her regular neighborhood leash walks. She will not bolt through your door but will sit or lie down when you ask her to, and most importantly of all, she will come when you call her, inside or outdoors. Your dog will also learn to relax on her bed when you need her to stay on her place for a time. Finally, you will find many other behavior problems have disappeared or decreased. But should any persist, we follow with a appendix to give you solutions for over 40 common dog problems.

Our first few lessons will introduce your dog to three new pieces of equipment. First is the training collar you have selected to attach a leash to. Your choices, as per Chapter 5, include a flat buckle collar, a Starmark collar, or a prong collar. See Chapter 5 for a review of those so you can decide which collar you want to start with. Remember, you can always start with one type of collar and later redo the exercise with a different kind if you were not satisfied with your dog's response. For example, some sensitive dogs will absorb the following lessons perfectly well wearing a plain buckle collar. However, rowdier or more excitable dogs may learn quicker and with less stress if they wear a Starmark collar. Still others may respond better to a prong collar. If you are unsure what will work best for your dog, start with a buckle collar. You can always repeat the lesson with a different collar if you are not satisfied that you made the right selection the first time.

The second piece of equipment is the leash itself. We'll start with a 6-foot leather or nylon leash. Third is the e-collar. You won't even need to turn the e-collar on initially. The purpose of placing it on the dog at first is simply to accustom your dog to wearing something new.

Before we begin, you will note that many of the lessons are short. Trainers know from experience that shorter training sessions done more frequently throughout the day are far more effective than doing one longer session. Follow the guidelines and you will be delighted at how quickly your dog begins to understand the exercises.

🐾 Keeping Track

Turn to the Lesson Planner on page 253 for a day-by-day breakdown of when each lesson should be introduced, repeated, and extended as needed.

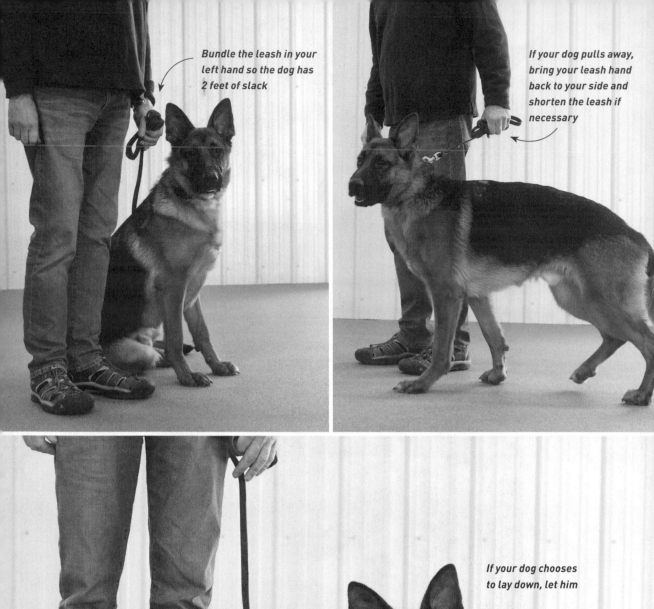

Bundle the leash in your left hand so the dog has 2 feet of slack

If your dog pulls away, bring your leash hand back to your side and shorten the leash if necessary

If your dog chooses to lay down, let him

Introduce the Training Collar

Approximate time: 5 minutes

How many times to repeat this lesson per day: 3

How many days to repeat this lesson: 1

Equipment: A 6-foot leather or nylon leash attached to the training collar of your choice. The e-collar will be on the dog, but you will not use it during this lesson.

Purpose of the lesson: ❶ To teach your dog not to pull on the leash, instead teaching your dog to leave slack in the leash; ❷ to teach your dog to occasionally check in by looking up at you without being prompted; ❸ to teach you how to educate your dog using your body language.

Location: Inside your home

A word about leash biting: As you begin training, a small percentage of dogs will become fixated on biting and tugging on the leash to the point where their attention cannot be refocused on the lesson. You can proceed through the lesson with a dog who plays only a little bit with the leash because those dogs will soon stop their shenanigans to pay attention to the lesson if you ignore the leash biting and persist. But a dog who completely obsesses on it will need a few preparatory lessons to curb leash biting before you proceed. Rub lemon juice concentrate on the area of the leash that your dog targets. Fill a small squirt bottle with lemon juice and, without reprimanding, squirt a few drops into your dog's mouth when he is grabbing at the leash. When your dog spits out the leash, say his name, and give him a treat when he looks at you. Better yet, if he knows how to sit, when he spits out the leash, ask for a sit and then give the reward with your dog in the sitting position. Most dogs will quickly learn to leave the leash alone and focus on earning rewards. After a few such prep lessons, you can resume teaching Lesson 1.

Note: At various times throughout the day and during some of your lessons, you will notice your dog choosing to lie down of his own volition. In the lesson notes you will find that this is usually permitted. As your dog lies down, it will be helpful if you simply say the word *down* as he is in the midst of doing it. Say it calmly and conversationally, because it is a fine idea for your dog to begin to associate the word with the action even before you teach the down as a lesson.

Remember, we never attach a leash to the e-collar. For many dogs we will recommend that you start this lesson with a Starmark training collar because it is easy to fit to your dog. When the collar is fitted correctly (snug around his neck so that it stays closer to his ears than to his shoulders) your dog cannot back out of it, and it is gentle but attention-getting when used as we'll describe. Plus, if your dog proves very sensitive to the Starmark collar, you can temporarily turn it inside out so that the plastic points do not touch your dog. But as we stated earlier, you may prefer to start with a flat or prong collar based on your dog's excitability level, sensitivity, and strength relative to yours.

A word about the primary objective of this lesson. You will teach your dog to stay close enough to you so the leash remains slack at all times. Keeping the leash loose is *your dog's responsibility.* This is not only the critical purpose of this lesson, but it is also a skill upon which we will build much of the coming training. You won't be able to train your dog if he constantly feels tension through the leash, which is exactly what happens when he pulls even a little bit. A taut leash causes the dog to resist and pull away even more than he already has, making things unpleasant for you. Further, the tension will mean that he doesn't have to look at or focus on you because he can feel that you're at the other end of that leash. Worst of all, your dog may become accustomed to the tension on his collar. He may never learn that there is another option, that there is a way to fix or prevent that, a way that is within his control. In fact, he's probably already at that point. The good news is that we're going to reverse

Your dog is doing his job by leaving slack in the leash

that and give your dog a job: to focus on you so that he can keep the leash loose and not feel tension on his body.

Simplified, there are two parts to training. First, your dog must focus on you to *see what you want*. Second, once he understands what you are asking, he must *want to do it*. Without these two factors, you will never have a trained dog. But with them, you'll not only be able to train your dog to reliably follow your commands, you'll also have a dog who tries to interpret what you need even before you ask.

It All Starts with a Loose Leash

We'll tell you here how to teach this lesson so that your dog can do his part. But you must also do your part, which is to make it possible for your dog to succeed at leaving the leash loose. Just a word of caution: you'll find this much easier to accomplish if you hold the leash in an easy-to-manage bundle in your left hand, which we will call your "leash hand." Keep that hand in a natural position, down at your side. Many people get a little nervous when practicing a leash exercise for the first time, and their leash hand unconsciously begins to rise in the air toward the chest. This is an unconscious reaction to a slight case of nerves. If you find that the leash becomes tight at any point in this or any subsequent lesson, glance down to see whether your dog is to blame or you are. If your hand has risen up beyond a natural position at your side, make a greater effort to keep it down in that natural position relatively near where your pants pocket would be. Your elbow will be only slightly bent, as it would naturally be when swinging your arms slightly during a walk. But your elbow will not be bent much more than that. If it is, *lower your leash hand.*

Let's get started.

1. Attach the leash to your dog's training collar and bundle it up in your left hand "accordion-style" so that the dog has 2 feet of slack when he is standing on your left side, quite close to you. Hold your leash hand down by your side as you naturally would when standing still, so as not to put tension on the leash from your end. Simply plant your feet and do not move them, even if your dog tries to wander off. If your dog is very large and usually pulls hard, you might want to stand with a wall on your right side for balance. The goal is for your dog to realize that he is wearing something new and that he will be more comfortable staying with you rather than leaving. Do not yank the leash. Just stand still. Be aware of your dog but do not stare at him. Your dog will learn more easily if you seem a bit detached rather than heavily focused on him with major eye contact.

2   Your dog may try to pull or walk away from you but will quickly realize that you are not going to follow. Your response is to keep your feet planted. Encountering the new form of pressure from the training collar, your dog will do one of several things:

- *Your dog steps away from you, feels the collar tighten slightly, then looks at you and steps closer to you.* This relieves the mild collar pressure. Your response should be a quiet word of praise at the exact moment your dog steps toward you. *Good dog,* or something to this effect, but not much more. Don't distract from the teachable moment. Shy or worried dogs may need you to say it quietly but enthusiastically. Excitable dogs will need these quick words of praise to be spoken calmly and quietly.

- *Your dog walks away from you, tightening the leash.* Rather than looking at you and stepping back toward you, the dog remains at the end of the leash for more than five seconds, obviously unsure what else he could do, or even straining to walk away from you. Your response is to keep your feet planted. Your leash hand will have been pulled out of position by the dog, so calmly bring your leash hand back to your side, bringing your dog back to you. This will relieve the collar pressure the dog created. You have helped your dog put a bit of slack back in the leash by bringing him back into position. If your dog is very strong, you might need to use two hands to help her back to your side, achieving a loose leash and no pressure from the collar. If your dog looks at you, praise. If she stays by you, even for a moment, praise again. Repeat this quiet process until your dog remains by your side for a few minutes.

- *Your dog tries to lie down.* If your dog decides to lie down, it simply means that he's willing to go along with your idea that he should remain close. Moreover, it means he is willing to self-calm and be relaxed. If necessary, let just enough leash slip through your fingers so the dog can lie down. If he remains close and quiet, you should stand still for the remainder of the 5-minute lesson. If he begins to roll around on the ground, tightening the

If your dog puts tension on the leash, plant your feet and bring him back to your side where the leash will be loose once again

leash, simply gather your leash back up to your original grip; take two steps forward, which will cause your dog to get up; and resume the lesson in the same way as before he lay down.

- *Your dog begins to jump on you.* Just as your dog jumps, maintain your grip on the leash so your dog has only a little slack, and pull the leash *straight up in the air* so that your dog receives a *slight* correction from the training collar while he does not have all four feet on the ground. *Instantly* lower the leash and resume the lesson. You may have to repeat again if your dog persists in jumping, but most dogs will readily stop. Quietly praise your dog after 5 seconds of no jumping. If praise causes your dog to jump again, repeat the process but praise more quietly.

- In the *highly* unlikely event that your dog seems to panic—thrashing and/ or vocalizing for more than an instant—stop the lesson and move down to a lower pressure training collar. Pay special attention to be sure you're not unintentionally raising your leash hand, putting unwarranted pressure on your dog. In later lessons, if the newly selected collar doesn't work well for you, you can probably go up one step with better results.

At the end of 5 minutes, your dog should be standing, sitting, or lying calmly by your side. The choice of which position to take is up to your dog. Certainly he will wonder what that was all about. But remember our objectives: First, the dog learns to keep a loose leash by staying close, not pulling away from you. Second, we want him to look at you occasionally. Teach calmly, with only a quiet word of praise spoken at those precise moments when your dog makes a good decision. You should repeat this lesson three or four times per day until both you and your dog find it easy. Once you have been able to perform three repetitions of Lesson 1 with the dog remaining relaxed by your side on a loose leash for the entire lesson, you are ready to move on to Lesson 2.

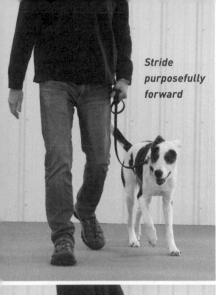

Stride purposefully forward

Begin your turn by pivoting abruptly

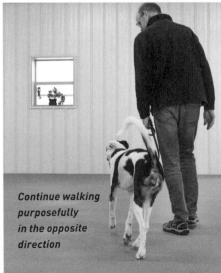

Continue walking purposefully in the opposite direction

Introduce the Purposeful Walk with the Training Collar

Approximate time: 10 minutes

How many times to repeat this lesson per day: 2

How many days to repeat this lesson: 3

Equipment: A 6-foot leather or nylon leash attached to the training collar of your choice. The e-collar will be on the dog, but you will not use it during this lesson.

Purpose of the lesson: ❶ To teach your dog to walk nicely by your side on a loose leash without pulling during the walk; ❷ to teach your dog to ignore light distractions; ❸ to teach your dog to occasionally check in with you by looking up at you without being prompted; ❹ to teach you how to educate your dog using body language.

Location: A room or hallway inside your home

Walk and Turn with Purpose

Whether using a large room, a set of rooms open to one another, or a long hallway, you'll purposefully walk from one end to the other. Imagine that you have a target at each end that you will walk briskly toward. You'll say nothing to your dog but step out at your quickest comfortable pace, walking to your target. This will cause your dog to pay close attention to your body language. Stand straight with shoulders back, chin up, eyes focused on your target rather than on your dog, and step out like a man or woman on a mission. Your goal is to walk all the way from your starting place, point A, to point B with your dog walking by your side on a loose leash, not pulling.

When you arrive at point B, you will immediately turn around without breaking pace and go right back to point A, where once again you will turn around without breaking pace and go back to point B. In other words, you will be *purposefully and briskly* walking in a continuous loop. If you walk with intention and commitment, your dog is much more likely to do exactly as you wish than if you dawdle. You know you're doing it right if someone were to look at you and think, "Wow! That person looks determined to get somewhere important." This holds true for all lessons which involve walking with your dog, especially the first few days you teach those lessons.

How you turn around is very important, so let's discuss that for a moment. Rather than making a big wide turn, you are meant to turn in place, essentially pivoting. Imagine an invisible path on the ground between your two points. Your feet should remain on or very close to that path at all times, *even when turning around.* This means your dog will have to adjust more to your position and direction than vice versa. It also means your dog will have to work just a little bit harder to stay with you, but your clarity of intent is much stronger when your body language instantly indicates which way you are going. A 180-degree turn makes that far clearer than a gradual loop, during which your dog may be thinking, "I wonder where we're going. It doesn't seem important." The precision of a 180-degree turn makes it instantaneously clear where you intend for the pack to go. Also understand that most dogs can turn on a dime, so you're not asking your dog to do anything especially difficult. We will call this 180-degree pivot an "about-turn."

The direction you turn—to your left or your right—is important for the sake of fluid motion. You have a dog on your left side and you are holding the leash in your left hand. At this stage, it will be far easier for you both if all of your about-turns are to your right, away from your dog. This will give your dog the outside position and will mean he has to take more steps and work a bit harder than you to complete the turn. This benefits you both. It's better mental exercise for the dog and it means you won't be tripping over him, which you might do if you turn around to your left. At this stage, it will be far easier and more educational for you both to turn around to your right.

How quickly you turn around is very important. In fact, it is essential to your dog's understanding of what you are trying to teach. Once you have arrived at the point

The Purposeful Walk begins with your dog standing or sitting next to you with slack in the leash

where you will make your 180-degree pivot, do so swiftly, purposefully, and without waiting for the dog. Most people have a tendency to wait for the dog or pause slightly right in the middle of that turn. It's a subconscious temptation, perhaps because you don't want to yank your dog. However, you must understand that your dog can always turn and move faster than you if he chooses to do so. If you pause even slightly during that turn, you will accidentally be sending the message that you wish for your dog to slow down or even stop. That would be the wrong message for you to send. You help your dog understand you much better if you hustle through that turn at your fastest comfortable walking pace. Don't run. Just walk briskly throughout the straightaways as well as the turns. The speed you should use is the fastest pace you can comfortably walk. That will vary according to your fitness level, but go as fast as you personally can without breaking stride to run. This is Purposeful Walking, and it will help your dog learn what you want because your body language suggests he should pay attention and focus on what you want, much as the African wild dogs follow their Pack Leader when she walks with intention.

Note: Your dog may begin to pull at some point during this lesson, maybe even immediately when you begin to walk. After all, he learned to remain by your side in the previous lesson, but only when standing still.

Let's get started:

1. Attach the leash to your dog and bundle it up in your left hand so that the dog has 2 feet of slack when he is standing right next to you. Hold your leash hand down by your side as you naturally would when standing still. At this point, your dog should remain relaxed by your side as he learned to do in Lesson 1. *If he is pulling and walking away from you, you should repeat Lesson 1 before moving on to Lesson 2.*

2. Start to walk, remembering the notes from above. As you move from point A toward point B, your dog begins to move ahead of you,

pulling on the leash. You should immediately, quickly, and *abruptly* turn around 180 degrees (staying on that imaginary line on the floor) and hustle back to point A. The effect on your dog will be that his pulling toward B is *swiftly* interrupted and he finds himself headed back the other way. That sudden 180-degree turn is the correction for pulling ahead of you and losing focus on you. Continue and repeat as needed. If you are turning abruptly enough on an appropriately chosen training collar, your dog will begin to walk at your side without pulling, hustling through the turns along with you. If your dog is still pulling by the end of 10 minutes, you may wish to repeat the lesson next time using a different training collar.

3. After a few of those abrupt right about-turns as your dog started to pull, he falls into line with the lesson and walks with you without pulling on the leash. In this case you continue the lesson; however, every 3 minutes or so you stop (anywhere on the route you choose) and remain still for about 30 seconds. Now you expect your dog to do what you taught him in Lesson 1: hold relatively still by your side on a loose leash. It is his choice as to whether he stands, sits, or lies down. However, if he begins to roll around, fiddle significantly, or jump, resume your point-to-point brisk walking and try 30 seconds of rest later. He'll soon understand that rest time is for quiet time rather than for chaotic behavior.

Some other behaviors your dog may exhibit:

- Some dogs will not rush ahead, pulling on the leash. Instead they will hold stock still, walk slower than you, sit, or even lie down. We call this going on strike. In most of these cases the dog is saying, "Nope. I'm not doing this." Your response should be simply to walk on. Ninety percent of dogs who do this behavior know from their prior experience with you that if they stop, *you'll stop too.* Now is the time to prove such a dog wrong. Keep moving, and

When you stop for a moment of rest, your dog should choose to calmly sit, stand, or lie down close to you

if you feel resistance on the leash as though your leash hand is being pulled behind you, *pick up your pace,* moving forward even faster. You may find it useful to pulse your hand forward a few times until your dog is moving, but do this *in motion.* Your dog will interpret this as effective urging to move forward. If you stop or slow down to urge your dog forward, either verbally or with the leash, the problem will worsen rather than improve. But if you do as suggested, in very short order your dog not only will learn that going on strike doesn't work but also that you have a countermove. Within a lesson or two, he'll stop going on strike and will walk nicely with you.

- A very few dogs may refuse to walk all the way to the very end of a room because they are worried about walking right up to a wall. If you believe your dog to be fearful, pick points that are more in the open and don't require him to walk right to a wall or other object that worries him.

- There is no coaxing your dog to walk with you during this lesson. You merely walk briskly. Take several short rest breaks or pauses during the lesson. Usually, 30 seconds to 1 minute will be enough.

- You should not talk to your dog during this lesson, except for a quiet and specifically timed word of praise now and again. The moments to praise are when your dog checks in with you by looking at you and when he makes a particularly well executed about-turn, especially if he previously struggled to keep up with your turns. If the praise immediately causes your dog to make a mistake, praise more quietly or stop talking altogether for that lesson.

- If your dog begins to jump on you during this lesson or bites the leash during rest, end the break and begin to walk and turn again. If that does not swiftly stop the problem, go back and repeat Lesson 1 until the behavior stops, then resume with Lesson 2.

At the end of 10 minutes, your dog should be walking by your side on a loose leash with 2 feet of slack. He should make the about-turns with you, and you should barely feel any pressure from the dog on your leash hand, even during the turns. When you slow down to stop, the dog should also slow down. And when you stop for a moment of rest, the dog should choose to calmly sit, stand, or lie down close to you. Again, if he wants to lie down, give him just enough leash to do that comfortably. Once you have been able to perform two repetitions of Lesson 2 with the dog walking relaxed by your side on a loose leash every day for 3 days in a row, you are ready to move on to Lesson 3.

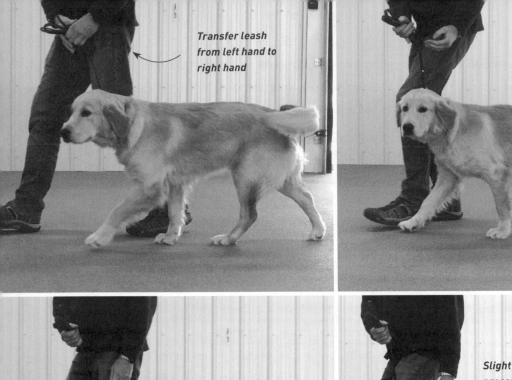

Transfer leash from left hand to right hand

Slight upward leash pressure as you come to a halt

Touch dog's hips with slight downward pressure

Teach Your Dog to Sit

Approximate time: 3 minutes

How many times to repeat this lesson per day: 4

How many days to repeat this lesson: 3

Equipment: A 6-foot leather or nylon leash attached to the training collar of your choice. The e-collar will be on the dog, but you will not use it for this lesson.

Purpose of the lesson: ❶ To teach your dog to sit using our specific method, because it will build reliability and duration in future lessons; ❷ to teach your dog that slight upward pressure on his training collar indicates he should sit; ❸ to teach your dog to reliably sit on your verbal command rather than waiting for a hand signal or treat, either of which he will probably ignore if distracted.

Location: Anywhere inside your home

Note: This lesson can be taught on the same days that you teach Lesson 2. Just do this lesson at different times. It won't take long. Do only three sits per lesson. Continue practicing this lesson until your dog reliably sits when you ask. You may have already taught your dog to sit, and you may have done that with treats or using a different method. Although it is beneficial that your dog already understands something about sit, we strongly suggest that you reteach it now according to our instructions. That's because our method will develop the teaching technique into a way of building a reliable sit despite distractions. Also, you may wonder why we didn't put sit as the first exercise as so many other dog training methods do. It's simple. Walking with your dog as per the prior lesson helps put your dog into pack drive. Therefore, it will be easier for him to learn the sit than if you had started it before walking with your dog.

1. Attach the leash to your dog's training collar. Have him on your left side. Hold the leash bundled up in your left hand so that the dog has only 6 inches of slack but the leash is not tight.

2. While taking a step forward, transfer the leash to your right hand, then stop and say *sit* simultaneously.

3. Stay by your dog's side, and *as you stop and say* sit, pull up slightly on the leash to create just a noticeable bit of upward pressure on your dog's neck while you simultaneously place your left hand on your dog's hips and gently touch downward. Do not push down hard. Most of the guidance for the sit should come from the upward pressure on the leash. This lifts the dog's head slightly. Being a quadruped, when his head is raised he will tend to understand he should put his butt on the floor. Your hand on his hips, *not on his back*, encourages him to do this. The instant your dog sits, release the upward leash pressure from your right hand and remove the downward hip pressure from your left hand.

4. Remaining in place by your dog's side where you have been the entire time, stand up straight. Transfer the leash from your right hand back to your left hand.

Note: Use peripheral vision to remain aware of your dog's position, but do not stare at your dog. If you lock eyes with your dog, even unconsciously, he will probably get up, thinking the exercise is over. If he immediately gets up, swiftly repeat the same sequence in place: right hand leash transfer, upward leash pressure, left hand gives slight downward hip pressure, and once the dog is sitting, transfer the leash again and stand straight up. All of this is done quietly and calmly with the dog by your left side.

5. Once your dog has remained sitting for about five seconds, simply say *let's go*, walk forward a step or two, then take a 30-second break before repeating.

Within 3 days, most dogs will begin to make the effort to sit themselves as you perform the steps in this lesson. Once that happens, you can stop the left-hand/right-hand leash transfer and simply lift the leash a little with the left hand if the dog does not quickly sit on command. You've eliminated the downward hip pressure. Once this is working well, say *sit* and do nothing. Count one Mississippi, and if the dog is not at least starting to sit, then raise the leash for upward pressure. Soon you should find your dog sitting reliably when you ask. When this happens, you should reteach the entire lesson from the very beginning but outside, where there will be more natural distractions. Within a day or so, the dog should sit when you ask, inside or outside.

If your dog sits but then starts to get up before you have said *let's go* to release him from the sit, lift the leash upward to re-sit your dog.

You may wish to proof your dog so that he will remain sitting for a longer period of time, even if you walk a short distance away from him and there are distractions in the environment. If so, please look at the sections on duration, distance, and distractions at the end of Lesson 10, which teaches the down. You can apply the same concepts to the sit. However, we believe that it is more comfortable for the dog to remain in position for a length of time if he is lying down. Either way, he does have to learn to ignore distractions.

You may wish to give your dog a treat for sitting. If so, here are a few tips:

- Give the treat while your dog is sitting.

- Place it right at your dog's nose so that he can remain sitting when he takes it.

- Use a very small treat so that it is gone quickly.

- If treats make your dog overexcited and frequently cause him to abandon the sit, then eliminate them.

- Within a few days make treats random. Give them less and less frequently, so that your dog tries ever harder to earn them by being a good sitter.

Give the treat while the dog is still sitting

Stride purposefully forward

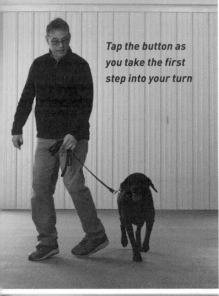

Tap the button as you take the first step into your turn

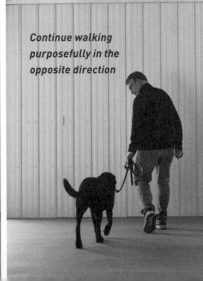

Continue walking purposefully in the opposite direction

Introduce the Purposeful Walk with the E-Collar

Approximate time: 10 minutes

How many times to repeat this lesson per day: 2

How many days to repeat this lesson: Minimum 2 days

Equipment: A 6-foot leather or nylon leash attached to the training collar of your choice. The e-collar will be on the dog, and the remote control will be in your hand.

Purpose of the lesson: ❶ To practice the skills learned in previous lessons; ❷ To teach your dog that a tap from his collar is a cue that you are both turning around to go the other way.

Location: A room or hallway inside your home

How to select a level: Be sure you have read the detailed discussion about e-collar types in Chapter 5 and levels in Chapter 6. If you are using an e-collar that has only 8 or 10 levels, you may find it difficult or impossible to achieve the subtle sensation we desire. To try to find a starting level on such a collar, we recommend you test it on your hand (see page 108). Note the first level you can feel with a quick tap on the constant button, then go *down* at least one level to start the lesson with your dog. If at any point during the training your dog seems upset, go down a level. If your dog seems upset on the lowest setting your e-collar offers, then we recommend you stop training until you get one of the e-collars we recommend in Chapter 5.

If using a Mini Educator, start the e-collar on level 6. Remember, a Mini Educator has 100 levels, so 6 is quite low. Most humans don't even feel it. This is a level that many dogs barely feel or don't feel at all. More importantly, it is a level that upsets very few dogs. For the next few lessons, we would rather err on the side of caution and have your dog barely feel the collar rather than feel uncomfortable. Eventually a comfortable yet effective educational level will emerge, and we will help you identify that.

1. As before, hold the leash in your left hand. You will probably find it easiest to hold the remote control in your right hand with the LED screen (if the remote has one) facing up, so that you can glance at it.

2. Repeat the targeted point-to-point walking pattern you established in Lesson 2. Although you're holding a new piece of equipment in your hand, remember to perform the same "shoulders back, chin up, eyes forward" Purposeful Walk as before. This time, however, you'll be using the e-collar to introduce the technology to your dog in a familiar, low-stress way that will eventually lead to off-leash reliability.

3. To use the collar, quickly tap and release the *constant* button at the same time as you take your first step into the about-turn. Just tap the button; don't hold it. Your timing is important. The idea is to tap and turn simultaneously. Be careful not to tap after you have already turned. Tap at the same instant you begin your turn.

You can now also introduce the e-collar as an additional cue for the sit. So you will tap the *momentary* button each time you stop and say *sit*. Remember, you should also lift your leash at the same time that you stop, say *sit*, and lift your leash. In Lesson 3, your dog learned to sit with most of these same cues. You probably were even able to stop lifting the leash to cue your dog to sit because he began to consistently sit when you stopped and said the word. Now, however, you are adding a new cue: the tap on the momentary button. Because you have made a small change to the command, your dog will benefit from the reminder provided by pulling up slightly on the leash. You will know you are making good progress on the *sit* command—and that your dog feels the e-collar—if, when your dog begins to wiggle or get up, you push the momentary button again, repeating the *sit* command, and he settles back into the sit, waiting for your next move.

If you have been diligent with your lessons up until this point, you might wonder why you even need to introduce the e-collar. Your dog may very well be walking and sitting nicely, at least indoors where we have started. Why can't we simply repeat these lessons outside and be done with it all? Where is the benefit in the e-collar?

What we seek to accomplish with the e-collar at this stage is merely introductory. To be frank, in the days before the current good e-collar technology was developed, the authors trained thousands of dogs using techniques very similar to what we have shared with you thus far. But even we eventually hit limitations in what we could accomplish with our training because we wanted—as you will want—to be able to trust that the dog's leash training will work equally well once we eliminate the leash. Yes, we always accomplished this with our own hand-picked and hand-trained dogs. But we are longtime professional dog trainers. Few clients reached the same reliability, especially near heavy distractions like rabbits or other dogs. It is the e-collar technique we are sharing with you here that will ultimately give you a happy, confident dog— unafraid of you or the equipment—who will still respond to you when off leash or distracted. And that gives you a dog you can enjoy more and keep safer.

So how do you know your dog is feeling the tap on the constant button when you turn? And how do you know he feels the tap on the momentary button when you ask him to sit? You might not, at least at first. Naturally, if you see any discomfort which occurs at the exact same time as you push the button, we advise you to lower the level. But we have picked level 6 as a starting point because the vast majority of the dogs we train either don't feel this level at all, in our professional opinion, or they feel it, but barely. We cannot remember a time when this level caused any dog in our care to vocalize, startle, jump, or otherwise indicate in any way that he was uncomfortable. Remember, if you inadvertently step on your dog's tail, he will yelp. If you accidentally clip a nail too short, he will whine. Dogs are transparent. A dog will tell you when he is uncomfortable. You should see no discomfort in your dog's aspect in this lesson.

In fact, it is entirely possible that level 6 will not be high enough for the dog to make the association we desire: that the quick little feeling from the collar means we are turning around if in motion or sitting when stopped. Some trainers advocate standing still with the dog, pushing the button on a low setting, and turning the e-collar up little by little until eventually the dog shows some sign that she feels it. Such signs may include flicking an ear or a rapid blink. And while a trainer with a highly trained eye might make this work, we find that the average dog owner with no e-collar experience can easily miss the very subtle cues a dog will give when she first detects the e-collar stimulation. And if that happens, the owner will probably go higher and use a level that the dog finds at least mildly uncomfortable. So we'll use a different method to pick a level the dog can detect but that doesn't worry her, what we call the educational level. On Day 2 of this lesson, let's do a little test to determine if your dog is feeling level 6, i.e., if you're using a Mini Educator. It's simple. Rather than walking all the way to point B, tapping the button as you turn back to point A, at some point during this lesson you will tap the button *when you're only halfway to point B* as you turn around and go back to point A. In other words, you're changing the game slightly by turning when your dog doesn't expect it. If your dog is not at all surprised by this change and if he easily makes this turn with you, chances are that he felt the level 6 tap which you gave him and understood that it meant "we're turning around now." However, if after trying a few unpredictable turns timed to simultaneously coincide with a tap, your dog is not synching easily with your turn, chances are you need to increase your level slightly. In this case, bump the level up to 8, teach the A to B tap and turn sequence all over again for a full day, and then try the random tap and turns the next day. When you have found the right level, not only will your dog—without concern—be unsurprised by the turn, but you will sense a greater precision in his turns. That is because he understands that a barely detectable tap means "we're turning around *now*."

Chances are you will need to turn the collar up from that initial level of 6 if you're using a Mini Educator. You may also need to turn it up if you are using a very low level with another brand. Yes, we want to start quite low, but ultimately we want to ensure that the dog is feeling the collar just as you felt it on your hand. Although some dogs feel and learn to respond easily to level 6, we have met many others who didn't feel or respond until level 12, 14, or even higher on the Mini Educator. Yes, you can read the number on the remote control, but it's more important to read the dog. Is she responding readily but without concern? That's what we're looking for.

Many people ask how they will know if the collar is set too high. Any vocalizing would make it obvious that the dog is uncomfortable. This is highly unlikely if you follow our directions. But what if your dog is not so uncomfortable that he would whine, but still the collar is set too high? In this case we would lower the collar level slightly and carry on with the lesson.

If the level is too high for the situation, your dog may startle every time you push the button, shake his head much more than usual, or constantly try to stop and scratch at the collar.

> **Note:** A quick word about scratching. Although constantly attempting to scratch at the collar can indicate that the level is a bit too high, it more often means the dog is indeed feeling the sensation, but it is new and feels like something that should be scratched, such as a flea. This is an especially common initial reaction in younger dogs and in muscular dogs with short, tight coats such as boxers. Before you determine that scratching indicates a level is too high, try working through the situation first. Do that by continuing to walk even though your dog wants to stop and scratch. *Do not stop.* Stopping to let your dog scratch an itch will give him the wrong idea. It will accidentally confirm for him that he can turn off the collar by scratching. On the other hand, if you just continue walking forward, he will soon realize that stopping to scratch is not going to be permitted, that there is no time for it. During this time, he will also become used to this funny new sensation and he will realize it wasn't an itch after all—it was a signal for him to turn around with you. Within one or two lessons he will magically stop trying to scratch.

Repeat this lesson until your dog is easily tapping and turning with you, sitting on command, and holding that sit for as long as you remain standing by his side. You may reward with a treat in the first series of repetitions, then randomize the treat. Once we have accomplished this in the home, perhaps even in two or three different locations in the home, we are ready to take an important step. We're ready to repeat and build on this training outside, where we will inevitably encounter many more distractions.

Marc teaches "sit" at the door because dogs are safer when they wait for permission to exit

Teach Your Dog to Sit at the Door

Approximate time: 5 minutes

How many times to repeat this lesson per day: 3 (plus any time you wish to take your dog outside through a door)

How many days to repeat this lesson: This should be your everyday practice from now on.

Equipment: A 6-foot leather or nylon leash attached to the training collar of your choice. The e-collar will be on the dog, and you will use it for this lesson.

Purpose of the lesson: ❶ To teach your dog to approach the door calmly; ❷ to teach your dog to sit while you open the door; ❸ to teach your dog to remain sitting until you give him permission to go through the door *with* you, not before you.

Location: Vary this lesson so that you are practicing at all the doors in your home that lead to the exterior of your dwelling, including the garage door if it is safe for your dog to be in the garage.

Note: This lesson is to be taught on the same days that you teach Lesson 4. Just do this lesson at different times. It won't take long. Do only three sits per lesson, and also practice the routine every time you want to walk your dog through the door from this point forward. You have already taught your dog to sit, but sitting at the door is harder, so we will also use the e-collar in conjunction with the *sit* command just as we did in the prior lesson. Although we are starting with *sit at the door*, you may begin to use it as needed to reinforce sit at any time if your dog refuses to do it on the first command, or if he gets up before you released him and you need to re-sit him.

It is very important that your dog learn to approach doors calmly and to sit until given permission to accompany you through the doorway. Most dog trainers who have been in the business for decades have received calls from clients because the dog has bolted through an open door. The authors received another of these calls just this week. The dog bolted out of an open garage door, ran down the street, and did not come when called. The owner was terrified. He chased after the dog, through traffic, until the dog got tired and allowed himself to be caught. Fortunately, this particular situation had a happy ending, but both of them could have been killed!

Before we begin this lesson, let's diagnose how door bolting begins and how many owners have accidentally contributed to it. Dogs naturally get excited when being taken outside. When a dog crowds the door, people worry they may step on a small dog. Or we worry that a big dog may crash into our knees. Or we are eager to get the dog out the door before he urinates. Regardless, we tend to approach the door with the dog already in an excited state of mind, especially if someone is knocking on the door. By the time we touch the knob, the dog is already crowding the door. Our tendency—and we do this without even realizing it—is to lean forward over the dog, ceding all the space around the door to the dog. Then we open the door when the dog is in front of us, with the dog literally anticipating where the door will crack open. As soon as we swing it open, the dog is charging through, whether on or off the leash.

No wonder so many people feel like walking the dog is a battle from the first step. That's because *the way you start an adventure is the way you will finish it.* If your dog leaps through the open door before you are ready, giving no thought to a mannerly exit, he'll likely be equally unfocused and excitable for much of the ensuing walk. If he learns to approach the door politely, sit as you open it, and wait for permission to calmly accompany you across the threshold, it is very likely that the rest of your walk can be an equally pleasant experience. In short, bolting through the door is no way to start a walk, let alone a lesson. The day before you begin to teach this lesson is the last day your dog will ever be permitted to charge through the door. Of all the lessons you have taught up to this point, this one will have the quickest payoff.

Let's begin:

1. The leash is attached to the training collar. The e-collar is on the dog. The dog is on your left side, and the leash is held bundled up in your left hand with about 6 inches of slack between you and the dog, remote control in your right hand. Set the e-collar to your dog's educational level. This is the level he feels at any given moment. It will be lower when he is calm. It will be at least a bit higher when he is excited. From a distance of at least 6 feet away, start a Purposeful Walk with your dog to the door, tap the constant button, then turn and go right back to where you started. Tap the momentary button as you ask your dog to sit. Repeat this process until your dog is turning easily away from the door and following you to where you will sit him.

2. Sit your dog at the door, being careful that the door will not hit him when you open it. You will find this lesson easiest if you do not actually stop to sit your dog when you are both facing the door head-on. You should be close enough to the door to easily reach the doorknob. It might be easiest if you stand sideways in relation to the door rather than facing it.

Note: When you open a door, it usually *swings* open, creating an imaginary arc on the floor. That arc starts at the bottom corner of the door's swing and continues all the way to the point where the door is fully opened. Imagine that arc on the floor. Be sure you sit your dog close to but outside the border of that arc. Otherwise you will hit him with the door as you open it. More than likely he'll see it coming and just scoot out of the way, but once you sit your dog we want him to understand that he should hold that sit until you release him from it by walking him through the door with you.

3. Pull the door open. If the configuration of the room and your door allow, you are actually positioned between your dog and the crack of the door when it is opened 6 inches. If your dog makes eye contact with you, give a treat with *yes*.

Open door while blocking your dog

Wait for eye contact before leading your dog through the door

4 Step through the door. If the dog moves through the doorway politely, give a treat the first couple of times as you sit him several feet past the threshold. Then fade the treat.

Your dog will go through the door with you, not ahead of you

Once you have begun to teach this lesson, you should never permit your dog to bolt out of a door ahead of you again. We understand that you may wish to relax certain rules with your dog as time goes on, and that's fine with us. We do the same with our own dogs. However, this particular lesson should have lifelong reinforcement. Crowding you at the door and rushing out ahead of you is now permanently off the table. As a side note, once your dog has learned this principle as relates to your home, you can also encourage him to sit and wait on the car seat as you open the door, rather than instantly leaping out of it without permission.

Eventually your dog will be able to obey this rule without equipment and without much insistence from you because it will become your dog's new default. For the time being, however, be prepared to reinforce the "door politeness" rule with the techniques and equipment you have used to teach the lesson. In the future, if your dog ever seems to forget the rule, just go back and reteach it, and you'll see how quickly you get obedience from your dog. Remember, this exercise is a major safety issue. It also bears repeating that the way your dog and you walk through the door determines so much of how the rest of the walk will go.

Remote right

Leash left

Remember: Walk with purpose!

If your dog pulls ahead, tap and turn

Purposeful Walking with E-Collar and Outdoor Distractions

Approximate time: 15 minutes

How many times to repeat this lesson per day: 2

How many days to repeat this lesson: Twice per day on most days for the rest of your dog's life.

Equipment: A 6-foot leather or nylon leash attached to the training collar of your choice. The e-collar will be on the dog, and the remote control will be in your hand. You may need to change to a slightly more corrective training collar.

Purpose of the lesson: ❶ To build on the skills learned in previous lessons; ❷ to teach your dog that the good leash manners established indoors are also required outdoors.

Location: A backyard, sidewalk, or area of your choice near your home. If you find some areas to be more challenging due to distractions, then use a lower distraction area for at least the first 2 days. As your dog becomes more reliable, practice in new places.

How to select a level: Start on your dog's normal educational level, the one that most often worked in Lessons 4 and 5 inside your home. However, because you are now practicing outdoors with more distractions, don't be surprised if you soon find that level to be less effective than it was indoors. Give it a few tries, but if your dog is overly excited and barely notices your turns, let alone your taps, then go ahead and slightly increase the level. Continue working, but you may need to repeat and adjust levels until you reach a number where—without overreacting—your dog notices the tap and begins to respond the same way he did indoors. Many dogs will not even notice the tap until it is higher than their indoor number. We can't tell you how much higher because that varies with each dog. But your dog will begin to respond well, realizing that you are merely repeating a lesson he already learned but in a new place. After that happens, keep an eye out for any eventual overreaction to the collar your dog might display. For example, if you jumped from an indoor 8 to an outdoor 13, you might find that after he has settled down and is performing the lesson he may flinch slightly at 13. This is a sign that you should lower the collar's setting until you again find a level that is neither too high for his comfort, nor too low for the situation. It may not be as low as his indoor level, but his calm outdoor level will probably be lower than his initial excited outdoor level. Pay more attention to your dog than to the number. If he is attentive and comfortable when you tap the button, he is telling you that everything is fine. If he starts to get jumpy, read that in his attitude and always be willing to lower the level.

Although you may have a preferred route for your normal walks, twice around the block for example, today's lesson will likely shorten that route. For the purposes of this lesson, it is *not important how far you walk*. It is important for you to focus on your dog *walking politely on a loose leash* for the entirety of your lesson. If you have budgeted 20 minutes for the lesson, it doesn't matter if you spend all of it walking from your mailbox to your neighbor's mailbox, tapping, and turning back. Teaching your dog to do it right matters far more than the distance at this stage.

Hold the leash bundled up in your left hand, connected to the training collar, with the dog on your left. Remember to hold the leash the same as you have in the prior lessons. By that we mean hold the leash so the dog has approximately 1 foot of slack. Hold the remote control in your right hand, a finger touching (but not pushing) the constant button. It is important that you not "string up the dog" by holding the leash too short. Some people accidentally do this by holding the leash shorter as they become nervous about the new and exciting change from indoors to outdoors. Also remember to keep your leash hand down by your left side so that you can swing it naturally as you walk. Make sure your left arm doesn't begin to magically rise in the air as you walk. Again, some people do that unconsciously if they get nervous.

It is more important than ever for you to remember how to help your dog by acting like a Pack Leader on a Purposeful Walk. We often tell our clients to be bold and confident; to walk like a New Yorker. If you have never been to New York, trust us when we say that means to walk briskly and confidently, as though nothing will get in your way or stop you. Keep your chin up and look ahead as you normally would when going for a walk. Although you may glance down at your dog from time to time, your vision should primarily be focused ahead of you. In other words, watch where you are going and don't stare at the dog. He'll take comfort from your confident attitude, and it will give him the idea that he should perform for you outside just as well as he has done inside.

Your neighborhood walks should be brisk and focused so your dog remembers good leash manners

For the duration of this lesson you will purposefully walk forward until you begin to notice your dog starts to forge ahead of you. At that moment you will tap the constant button and briskly turn around, pivoting in place as you did in your home. After the turn, walk 10 or so feet and turn around again. If your dog is not pulling, if your dog is walking attentively at your side without tightening the leash, continue your walk in your original direction.

If your goal is to walk around the block, you may be able to do that with a few taps and turns on your first lesson. If not, don't worry. Many people will need to spend the first 10 minutes of the lesson finding the right levels. They may need to make so many turns that they don't make it very far from their own front door. Don't worry. This is normal. It may take you a few lessons before you can actually complete your desired route without constantly turning around. It's not how far you go that is important. How well your dog walks is the object lesson. The distance will increase lesson by lesson.

Here are a few points to bear in mind:

- Allow your dog a moment to sniff and eliminate at the beginning, middle, and end of the lesson. However, do not stop to allow your dog to sniff every spot during the rest of the lesson. If your dog truly has to eliminate, of course you stop and permit that. But most dogs have learned the walk is a pull-a-thon and a sniff-a-thon. Do not permit that idea or behavior to persist.

- Here's how to stop your dog from stopping to sniff everything. If your dog tries to stop when you know he doesn't really have to potty, don't break stride. *Keep moving.* At the exact moment you feel resistance from the leash, maintain your own forward motion and give the button a quick tap. It won't take long before your dog agrees to wait for those pit stops you'll give him.

- Lesson time is not the moment to stop and let people pet your dog or to let their dog meet yours. Keep walking and toss a "Sorry, we're training" over your shoulder as you go. Don't stop!

- Occasionally stop and practice a sit when you sense your dog might be getting tired and would benefit from a brief moment of rest.

- If your dog likes treats, during a calm sit is a good moment for a treat to magically appear down at his nose. Prepare ahead for that moment so you don't disturb the calm by digging around in your pocket for a treat.

- If your dog wishes to lie down during the sit, we recommend you let out just enough leash to permit that, provided it's a safe spot.

An Important Note About Lesson 6

This is the lesson that teaches your dog to observe excellent leash manners when outside on your daily walks. Although you make time for potty and a bit of rest, you should observe the principles of this lesson—and so should your dog—for the rest of his walks . . . always. Within a few weeks, you will find less need to be conscious of all the steps you used to teach this lesson. Eventually you will be able to let your dog have more say about when and where he stops for a quick sniff. However, never again will you permit your dog to pull without using the system you have learned. Although most dogs will need the occasional reminder, good leash manners are forever!

Note: For the next few weeks, tap the button on your dog's educational level whenever you stop to sit your dog or make a turn. This is simply a reminder to your dog to pay attention. Eventually walking politely by your side will become your dog's new default and you can fade back on the reminder taps, but wait a few weeks for the good behavior to become the new norm.

Finally, remember that dogs need adequate mental and physical stimulation on a daily basis to feel fulfilled. Twice-daily Purposeful Walks, for a *minimum* of 15 to 20 minutes each, are the outlet your dog most needs to bond with you as his Pack Leader. They also enable him to reduce or stop problem behaviors. When weather and time permit, go for longer walks. We highly recommend that you take two such walks a day for the rest of your dog's life, starting from the day you first teach this lesson. We promise you'll reap enormous benefit if you do.

Hold leash and remote in your left hand while walking forward

Simultaneously call your dog and tap the button as you move backward

Move the treat up as you tell your dog to sit

Introduce Coming When Called Inside the Home

Approximate time: 3 minutes

How many times to repeat this lesson per day: 3 to 5

How many days to repeat this lesson: 3 days minimum; you can practice Lesson 7 right before and after your two daily leash walks as taught in Lesson 6.

Equipment: A 6-foot leather or nylon leash attached to the training collar of your choice held in your left hand. The e-collar will be on the dog, and the remote control will also be in your left hand, a finger ready on the constant button. You will hide a small treat in your right hand.

Purpose of the lesson: ❶ To teach your dog to turn around and come to you when you call; ❷ to teach your dog that sometimes you will require him to ignore a distraction and come to you; ❸ to show your dog that coming when called is not optional, but it is rewarding.

Location: Random areas inside your home; vary the locations.

How to select a level: Start on your dog's normal educational level, the one that most often worked in Lessons 4 and 5 inside your home. You may need to lower or increase the level depending on your dog's response.

Note: This lesson is to be taught on the same days that you teach Lesson 6. Just do this lesson at different times. It won't take long. Practice no more than three recalls per lesson so that it remains fun and does not become repetitious to your dog. But do practice it sufficiently for your dog to become very familiar with the exercise.

The first few times you teach this lesson, you will hold the leash bundled up in your left hand as you have done for the walking and sitting lessons, except the remote will also be in your left hand. You do not need to start this lesson with your dog sitting. Walk forward as you have done in various other lessons inside the home. But at some random point, rather than make an about-face, you will do *three things at the same time*:

1. Say your dog's name and the word *come*. Say it with a happy tone. Don't try to sound like a "dog trainer," yell, or sound angry, or your dog may be reluctant to come to you. Be your calm and collected self rather than seeming overexcited lest your dog think you want to play. We want you both calm and focused.

2. Give a fast tap of the constant button.

3. Switch directions from walking forward to backward. Imagine that you had been walking forward on a chalk line along your floor. With your dog at your side as usual, you will smoothly and *quickly reverse your direction so that you remain walking on the chalk line,* but now you are walking backward. As you walk backward, reach out to *hold the treat well in front of you and downward, almost touching your dog's nose* with the treat in your right hand. Continue walking backward, and stop after 6 to 8 feet, bringing the treat to your knees and then up as you tell your dog to sit. Provided your dog sits, immediately give your dog the treat *when he is in the sitting position.* Have your dog hold that sit position for up to 10 seconds while you very quietly praise. If your dog attempts to get up before you release him, lift the leash as in the sit lesson and repeat the *sit* command. Reduce tension on the leash when your dog sits again, but this time eliminate the verbal praise so he doesn't get excited and move. After a short sit, release your dog by saying his name and *let's go.* Walk a step forward to get him up and moving out of the sit. This repetition of the exercise is now complete. Break off and relax for a moment, then repeat somewhere else in your home.

Points to remember when starting the *come* command:

- As your dog begins to get the hang of the recall, start to hold the leash more loosely, slowly *allowing your dog to get farther ahead of you* before you tap the button and call him. Work up to only holding the handle of a 6-foot leash so that he can get well in front of you. Eventually you will be calling him when he is far from you, so as he learns, allow him to get in front a few feet before you call him.

- If the tap seems to upset him, lower the level. If he doesn't even notice it, increase the level. The correct response to the e-collar tap should be a happy recognition that a turn/walk toward you for 6 to 8 feet/sit sequence is about to happen, quickly followed by a treat, praise, or both.

- Use a treat that your dog *really* likes. It should be very small, about the size of a pea, to keep your dog motivated to work for more. If your dog isn't very food motivated, try a super high-value treat such as chicken breast and practice before rather than after meals. If your dog doesn't care about treats at all, just supplement sincere and calm praise with a gentle touch.

- Many people have a tendency to raise the treat, stop walking backward, and sit the dog almost immediately after reversing direction. Remember to clear an area in your home and *walk backward for a significant distance*, at least 6 feet. Eventually you'll need your dog to recall to you from far away, which means he'll be approaching you for a long time, and this is what we are beginning to teach here.

Once you have practiced this lesson for a few days you'll probably find that your dog anticipates what you are going to do. You'll tap, walk backward, and then he will turn, follow, come to you, and sit for his treat. As he begins to understand the sequence and comply easily, begin to randomize the treat. Don't give him the treat every time, maybe every second or third time. When you walk backward, do still hold out your hand and lure him in even when you don't have a treat. This is turning into a hand signal. In place of the treat, you can give quiet verbal praise or a brief, calm pat. But do everything else the same.

Walk purposefully toward the food with leash and remote in your left hand

Tap button and call the dog

Walk backward luring the dog to you with treat in your right hand

Raise the treat and ask your dog to sit

Give your dog the treat while he is in the sit position

Using Distractions to Build Reliability for the Indoor Recall

Approximate time: 5 minutes

How many times to repeat this lesson per day: 3

How many days to repeat this lesson: 3; you can practice Lesson 8 right before and after your two daily leash walks as taught in Lesson 6.

Equipment: A 6-foot leather or nylon leash attached to the training collar of your choice held in your left hand. The e-collar will be on the dog, and the remote control will also be in your left hand, a finger ready on the constant button. You will hide a small treat in your right hand.

Purpose of the lesson: To teach your dog the importance of coming when called even when he is mildly to moderately distracted.

Location: Random areas inside your home. Vary the locations.

Most dogs will understand and easily comply with Lesson 7 within 2 or 3 days. Once the recall, as described above, becomes almost too easy, it is time to introduce a distraction into the mix. After all, the times you will most need your dog to pay attention to your recall command are when he least wants to do it, such as when he is chasing a squirrel toward the street. Here is a process to help you create a distraction in the home so you can begin to condition your dog to come when you call, even if he doesn't initially want to.

Take a food storage container lid or paper plate and place it on the floor right at the point where you will reverse direction and call your dog. Hold the leash bundled up in your left hand, with the dog on your left side. Walk your dog close to the plate. Have one of his favorite treats in your hand and let him see you put that treat in the center of the plate, but don't let him eat it. Briefly ignore any pulling he might do at that moment, but do hold him back, away from the treat. Then turn away from the paper plate and have him walk with you away from it. Hold a second treat hidden in your right hand, leash and remote held in your left hand. A good distance to walk would be 10 feet. Turn back toward the plate with the treat on it.

Even though you have previously allowed your dog to get up to 6 feet ahead of you before reversing directions and calling him, it will be harder this time because we have introduced a distraction. So, for the next few sessions, you will hold the leash bundled up, with the dog feeling no tension but unable to get very far in front of you without tightening up the leash. Begin to walk toward the paper plate. You will tap the button, reverse, and call your dog (the same way you have been practicing) when one of the following happens: one, he lunges ahead of you to get to the treat, tightening the leash; or two, he walks politely with you to within 2 feet of the plate.

Most dogs will pull toward the paper plate. If that happens, you will immediately tap the constant button, reverse, and call your dog, walking backward, hand held out with the treat down to his nose, then ask for the sit. If your dog heavily resists you, then just tap the button a second time—as you continue walking backward—and you may even give the dog a quick tug toward you as you remain in motion, reversing away from the dog. If you practiced the routine sufficiently before introducing the paper plate, your dog will very quickly respond correctly to you. If not, go back and practice more without the treat, then come back to this part of the lesson.

A Note About Levels: Be aware, once distractions are involved, you may need to raise the e-collar level a little bit. If you raise the level, do it slowly until you find the level where your dog responds but does not show discomfort. Also be aware that, once he calms down, you may need to lower the level again.

If your dog started to pull away from you but then quickly reoriented when you tapped the button, reversed direction, and called, then once he is sitting in front of you, let him briefly sniff the treat you hid in your hand, but do not let him eat it. Immediately repeat the exercise. In very short order he will remain attentive to you when you tap, reverse, and call, thus earning the treat from your hand. But let's assume that you walk your dog close to the paper plate, but before he can get to eat the treat off it, you tap and walk backward. Like most dogs who have been well prepared with practice, he comes, then sits right in front of you, earning the treat from your hand. Immediately after you have fed him that treat, walk him right up to the paper plate and let him eat that treat, even if you have to point to it, giving him permission. If he tries to pull you to the plate, then just do some taps and turns as you initially did in Lesson 4 until your dog walks politely up to the paper plate, where you can give him permission to eat the treat.

We want your dog to learn that, once you have called him, he must ignore any tempting distraction. He should drop whatever he was doing, then he should immediately turn and come to sit in front of you. As you practice this lesson, your dog will come to understand that responding to your call is not

Your dog will learn that the recall is not optional, but it is rewarding

optional, but it is rewarding. He'll also learn that sometimes you will give him the treat as a bonus. Once your dog demonstrates understanding, be sure to start giving both the initial reward as well as the paper plate reward randomly. Once a dog understands an exercise, science and experience show that random reward is always more powerful than constant reward.

Before We Teach This Lesson Outside . . .

Most dogs love to be outdoors. And why wouldn't they? We humans can only imagine how much scent is in the air and on the ground. How lucky to have a dog's nose, 10,000 times more powerful than our own! They want to investigate

Stride purposefully toward the treat

Vary the exercise by letting your dog eat the treat and then call him back to you

everything they smell, see, and hear. That means you will be competing with Mother Nature and the environment as you begin to teach the *come* command outdoors and, eventually, from greater distances. So before you do that, once your dog is consistently successful indoors, be sure to repeat the paper plate lesson with a few variations. Here are a few that we can think of, but feel free to invent some of your own.

- Vary the location of the plate. Use different areas of your home, a friend's house, and the garage if it is safe.

- Vary the type of treat on the plate. Use a few crumbs of bacon to really up the ante.

- Use plates of different sizes and colors.

- Prop your front or back door open and put the plate right on the threshold, but keep a good grip on the leash!

- Occasionally use a favorite toy instead of the paper plate. The reward after training is to play with the toy.

Be understanding and patient, but also be consistent. When you introduce effective distractions, your dog may very well act like he has forgotten the exercise which he had been performing nicely. But trust us, he hasn't forgotten. He is distracted. We don't think of this as a problem. This is your *opportunity*, a chance to teach him again under circumstances that better resemble real-world conditions. Simply persist and teach the lesson again as described here until your dog will recall to you quickly and happily, regardless of the increasingly tempting indoor distractions. Your dog is learning that you will eventually let him eat those bacon crumbs (or whatever delicious temptations you have put on the plate), but he is also learning that he must *earn* them by coming when called.

When this becomes consistently easy, let's teach the lesson again, but outside, where we will truly need it.

Tap button as you change directions and walk backward

Continue walking backward for 6 to 8 feet

Lift treat and ask your dog to sit . . .

. . . and give him the treat

Introduce Coming When Called Outside the Home

Approximate time: 3 minutes

How many times to repeat this lesson per day: 2 to 4

How many days to repeat this lesson: Continue to practice this lesson during your two daily leash walks. Do so at least until you begin Lesson 11, at which point you can integrate it right into Lesson 11. You may find it beneficial to continue practicing this lesson all the way through Lessons 12 and 13, until your dog's outdoor recall becomes very reliable, even with distractions present.

Equipment: A 6-foot leather or nylon leash attached to the training collar of your choice held in your left hand. The e-collar will be on the dog, and the remote control will also be in your left hand, a finger ready on the constant button. You will hide a small treat in your right hand.

Purpose of the lesson: ❶ To begin teaching a reliable recall outside the home; ❷ to teach your dog that sometimes you will require him to ignore moderate to strong distractions and come to you; ❸ to show your dog that coming when called is not optional, but it is rewarding.

Location: If you have a backyard, this is a good place to start. Otherwise, start with any outdoor location which is very familiar to your dog. You can even use a familiar sidewalk, or you can practice along the route which you have been using for your repetitions of Lesson 6, walking with an e-collar and outdoor distractions. As your dog becomes more reliable, start practicing this lesson in new locations.

How to select a level: Start on your dog's normal educational level, the one that most often worked in Lesson 7 when inside your home. You may need to lower or increase the level depending on your dog's response.

The first few times you teach this lesson, you will hold the leash bundled up in your left hand, except the remote will also be in your left hand. You do not need to start this lesson with your dog sitting. Walk forward as you have done in various other lessons inside the home. At a moment when your dog is mildly distracted, you will do *three things at the same time*:

1. Say your dog's name and the word *come*. Say it with a happy tone. Don't try to sound like a "dog trainer," yell, or sound angry, or your dog may be reluctant to come to you. Be your calm and collected self rather than seeming overexcited, lest your dog think you want to play. We want you both calm and focused.

2. Give a fast tap of the constant button.

3. Switch directions from walking forward to backward. Imagine that you had been walking forward on a chalk line along the ground. With your dog at your side as usual, you will smoothly and *quickly reverse your direction so that you remain walking on the chalk line,* but now you are walking backward.

As you walk backward, reach out to *hold the treat well in front of you and downward, almost touching your dog's nose* with the treat in your right hand. Continue walking backward, and stop after 6 to 8 feet, bringing the treat to your knees and then up as you tell your dog to sit. Provided your dog sits, immediately give your dog the treat *when he is in the sitting position*. Have your dog hold that sit position for up to 10 seconds while you very quietly praise. If your dog attempts to get up before you release him, lift the leash as in the sit lesson and repeat the *sit* command. Reduce tension on the leash when your dog sits again, but this time eliminate the verbal praise so he doesn't get excited and move. After a short sit, release your dog by saying his name and *let's go*. Walk a step forward to get him up and moving out of the sit and continue your walk.

Points to remember when starting the *come* command outside:

- As your dog begins to get the hang of the outdoor recall, start to hold the leash looser, slowly *allowing your dog to get ever farther ahead of you* before you tap the button and call him. Work up to only holding the handle of a 6-foot leash so that he can get well in front of you. Eventually you will be calling him when he is far from you, so as he learns, allow him to get in front a few feet before you call him.

- If the tap seems to upset him, lower the level. If he doesn't even notice it, increase the level. The correct response to the e-collar tap should be a happy recognition that a turn/walk toward you for 6 to 8 feet/a sit sequence is about to happen, quickly followed by a treat, praise, or both.

- Use a treat that your dog *really* likes. It should be very small, about the size of a pea, to keep your dog motivated to work for more. If your dog isn't very food motivated, try a super high-value treat such as chicken breast and practice before rather than after meals. If your dog doesn't care about treats at all, just substitute sincere and calm praise with a gentle touch.

- Many people have a tendency to raise the treat, stop walking backward, and sit the dog almost immediately after reversing direction, especially when outside. Keep moving. Remember to look behind you before you recall your dog and *walk backward for a significant distance*, 8 to 10 feet if you can. Eventually you'll need your dog to recall to you from far away, which means he'll be approaching you for a long time.

As he begins to understand the sequence and easily complies, begin to randomize the treat. Don't give him the treat every time, maybe every two or three times. When you walk backward, do still hold out your hand and lure him in, even when you don't have a treat. This is turning into a hand signal. In place of the treat, you can give quiet verbal praise or a brief, calm pet. But do everything else the same way.

Hold the treat to the dog's nose while he is sitting

Lower the treat to the floor

Allow the dog to eat the treat in the down position

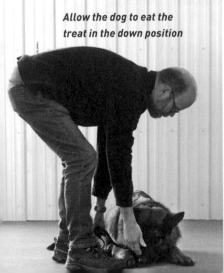

Introduce the Down

Approximate time: 3 minutes

How many times to repeat this lesson per day: 3 to 5

How many days to repeat this lesson: 7 days minimum, but this is an exercise you will want to occasionally practice until it has become extremely reliable. You can practice this lesson every day when convenient. Good moments include when you are watching TV or right after you finish practicing the Purposeful Walking exercises in the following lessons.

Equipment: A 6-foot leather or nylon leash attached to the training collar of your choice held in your left hand. The e-collar will be on the dog, and the remote control will be in your left hand with the leash. Have a finger ready on the constant button. Hold a treat hidden in your right hand.

Purpose of the lesson: To teach your dog to lie down on command.

Location: Start this lesson in your home, preferably on a smooth surface such as a wood or tile floor, because your dog will be less able to brace himself to resist lying down. The exception occurs if you have a very thin-coated dog and you are starting this lesson in winter, when the smooth floors will be cold. In that case, you may prefer to start on carpet. That being said, after a few days, begin to vary locations within the home and, if weather permits, outside the home in quiet areas. When you eventually move outside, avoid asking your dog to lie down on cold, wet surfaces or on prickly types of grass, especially if your dog is short-coated.

How to select a level: Start on your normal educational level, the one that most often worked for you in Lesson 7, inside your home. You may need to lower or increase the level, depending on your dog's response.

Note: At various times throughout the day, and even during some of your lessons, you will notice your dog chooses to lie down of his own volition. As your dog lies down, it will be helpful if you simply say *down* as he is in the midst of doing it. Say it calmly and conversationally, but it is a fine idea for your dog to begin to associate the word with the action, even before you teach the down as a lesson. We have waited until fairly deep into the lesson plan to teach the down because your dog will learn it much faster and easier once you have reached an understanding. You are now dealing with a calmer dog. However, for the time being, avoid practicing the down near intense distractions, such as running children or other pets.

1. Start with your dog in the sitting position. You may find it more comfortable if you kneel or sit in a chair next to your dog. Your position should be alongside your dog, with both of you facing the same direction.

2. The dog is on your left. The leash and remote control are held in your left hand. You have a finger poised on the constant button. A treat is concealed in your right hand. Use a better-than-usual treat, such as a small bit of chicken or a tiny cube of cheese.

3. Hold the leash bundled up tightly in your left hand but not so tightly as to put tension on your dog's collar.

4. If at any point your dog should stand up, stop what you are doing and re-sit him. Use the gentle upward leash pressure combined with a tap of the constant button, similar to the way you taught him during the lesson on sit.

5. With your dog sitting by your side, calmly do all of the following *at the same time:*

- Say *down.*
- Tap the constant button once.

- Bring the treat to (nearly touching) your dog's nose.

- Begin to pull the leash down, slowly placing *minor* downward pressure on your dog's training collar.

- Slowly lower the treat from your dog's nose to his toes, or you may simply point to the ground.

1. Ideally your dog will yield to the leash pressure, following the treat to the floor. Open your fingers, allowing your dog to eat the treat the moment he lies down, but not before.

2. Loosen any pressure on your dog's neck by releasing only a couple inches of leash, so that your dog feels comfortable lying down and is not pinned to the floor. Depending on your body position, you may find it easiest to step on the leash to arrest any attempt your dog may make to get up before you release him. Just be sure there is a little slack between the leash and the dog's training collar.

3. Very quietly and calmly, praise your dog with a simple *good dog*. (Excited praise will cause your dog to get up prematurely.)

4. Keep your finger ready on the constant button, and if your dog should begin to get up before you release her, tap the button as you use the leash to settle her again into the down. Ideally you would do this before your dog is all the way up.

5. Once your dog is down, silently count to five and then release her by saying *let's go* and walking a step forward.

We know this sounds like a lot of steps, but once you get the hang of it, you'll see that most of them are easy and natural to do simultaneously in one smooth movement. If it seems intimidating at first, put your dog away and practice a few times with an imaginary dog. Just don't let the neighbors see you!

Reducing the Number of Cues to Make the *Down* Command More Reliable

You must take into account several factors to progress the down so that your dog lies down on a single request and stays down for as long as you need. Here are the issues you should bear in mind:

- At first you are guiding your dog into the down with many cues, which include saying *down*, the downward leash pressure, the tap of the button, and the treat the dog follows to the floor.

- Although your dog will likely need all these cues for a while, the more you practice, the easier it will become for your dog to comply with the command. So, after the first few days, delay the downward tug on the leash but do everything else. He'll probably lie down anyway. If he doesn't, just apply the leash pressure slightly more abruptly than before, which says to the dog, "You know this. Don't wait for the leash pressure."

- One by one you'll be able to delay, and then eliminate, most of the other cues. Eventually you should be able to down your dog by pointing to the ground with the same hand motion you used to create the downward leash pressure. Now you have a hand signal. If needed, tap the button should you have to repeat the command a second time. After a week of practice, should your dog get up before you release him, using the educational level, hold the constant button down as you take the leash close to your dog's collar and pull straight down, helping him back into the down position. Be sure to release the button just as your dog downs again. If he seems upset by the e-collar, lower the level.

- Once you get to the point where your dog complies easily with the down, you should not only delay treats but make them random. In other words, don't give a treat every time. Make them less and less frequent. But when you do use them, make sure to place the treat between your dog's front paws *while he is lying down* so that he is reinforced into the down rather than tempted out of it.

Adding Duration, Distance, and Distractions to Make the Down Really Useful

Down is one of the most useful commands you can teach your dog. If he does it reliably, you can use this command so your dog can be near you at dinner time without begging. If you break a glass, you can use the down to keep your dog safe while you clean up. And if your dog can be counted on to perform a solid down, you can take him to an outdoor café and let him relax by your table while you enjoy a meal or a coffee. But for that to happen, you'll need your dog to hold the down for a longer period of time than the five seconds we started with. You'll also need him to lie down and stay while you move farther away from him. And you'll certainly need him to ignore distractions while he remains committed to his down-stay.

Once your dog will consistently lie down on a single verbal command combined with the hand signal we have described, you are ready to begin adding three factors that will ultimately make the *down* command not only reliable but also really useful. The factors that you will add into the training mix are duration, distance, and distractions. You will add these factors *one at a time*, and you must practice each of them for a substantial period of time until they become easy for your dog. At first, each will be difficult, but we have set up the training system so that you'll be able to easily clarify any confusion for your dog.

> **Note:** Each of the techniques that follows can be used to add distance-, duration-, and distraction-proofing to the *sit* command in the event that your dog is not yet fully reliable at holding the sit.

ADDING DURATION TO THE DOWN

Down is a position, but it is not very useful unless your dog will hold the position for a duration of time determined by you, not the dog. Let's get this question out of the way first: should you say *stay* and give a stay hand signal once your dog is down?

We believe that is not necessary because you can make the *stay* command part and parcel of the down. You'll show your dog that he is to hold that down until you release him from it, much as you release him from a sit. That being said, we believe no harm will be done if you wish to add the word *stay* and a hand signal right after the dog lies down.

Note: If you choose to add the word *stay*: Say *only* the word *stay*. Do not say your dog's name before or after that word, because it may cause him to think you want him to get up. At the same time that you say *stay*, briefly hold the flat palm of your hand in front of your dog's nose without touching him. Hold that signal for no more than one second lest your dog think it an invitation to lick or play. Remove your hand and stand straight up.

Regardless of whether you choose to say *stay* or not, here are a number of steps you must take to add duration to the down.

1. Once your dog is down, remain by his side but stand up straight. Be sure to let out enough leash so that the dog feels no tension on his training collar. We will add distance (from you) later. But right now we are working only on extending the length of time he holds the down.

2. Keep a finger poised on the momentary button. If you need to tap it, you won't have time to fumble around looking for it.

3. Look away from your dog. *Do not lock eyes with him* or he will likely think you want him to do something other than what he's already doing.

4. Remain aware of your dog by frequently using your peripheral vision. If he shifts his weight to get more comfortable, you will have no reaction. But if he wiggles as though he is going to get up, tap the momentary button and say *down*. If he does not immediately settle back into the down, smoothly reach down for the leash, tap the button one last time, and help him down using quick downward leash pressure.

5. Sometimes it can be helpful to move around your dog in a tight circle when he is learning to extend the down-stay.

6. Count silently and slowly to 10. That is how long you want your dog to hold the down. It is double the time of his first down lessons. Release him by saying his name and *let's go*. Take a step or two forward and calmly encourage your dog to go with you.

7. Praising for duration of the down is tricky. At this stage, adding food or verbal praise may cause excitement, which can lead to confusion, thus causing the dog to get up prematurely. We advise you to praise with a quiet word and touch after the exercise is completed. Don't use food treats after the release or your dog may want to end subsequent downs early to get a treat.

8. You should add more time to the down only when your dog can perform five perfect repetitions of the down for 10 seconds. This means five repetitions during which you did not need to correct your dog back into the down. After he has mastered the 10-second down, extend to 30 seconds, then 60 seconds, then 90. Continue until your dog will hold the down perfectly for 3 to 5 minutes.

ADDING DISTANCE TO THE DOWN

Eventually it will be important for your dog to understand that once you have told him to lie down, he is to hold that position even if you move away from him. When we first begin to add distance to the down, remember to temporarily reduce duration. Because it will be harder for your dog to hold the stay once you step away from him, we'll decrease duration for a little while to help him learn distance without confusion. Here is how you add distance to the down.

1. Down your dog on your left side. After the brief down hand signal and verbal *down* command, stand up straight.

②   Create some slack in the leash by letting a foot of it slip through your hand.

③   Repeat the verbal *down* command without locking eyes with your dog and take one side step to your right, away from your dog. You are stepping to the side, rather than stepping forward, to give your dog a hint that he is not to follow.

④   If your dog gets up, immediately push the constant button as you step back to him, say *down*, and help him back into position with downward leash pressure.

⑤   After about 10 seconds, sidestep back one step left, which puts you back into your original position.

⑥   Wait about 5 seconds, then release your dog.

Perform the above process until you can take several steps to the right, backward, or forward. Be very sure you do not tug on the leash when you take those steps. Keep your leash slack. Be careful to put no upward or sideways leash pressure on your dog when you want him to stay down. Slowly add back duration, a little bit at a time, as your dog shows increased understanding that you can move but he must not. Do remain aware of his body language. If he shifts his weight to get comfortable, do nothing. However, if he begins to get up, from wherever you are, tap the momentary button, saying *down* at the same time, and calmly grasp the leash *close to where it attaches to the collar*, helping your dog back down with quick downward leash pressure. Then release your grip on the leash and remain by your dog's side until the next repetition.

Note: If you do have to move back to your dog to correct an error if he gets up prematurely, move back to him smoothly. Don't lock eyes with him. Don't lunge at him. And don't make any scolding noise at him. Any of those will merely confuse or upset your dog.

Within a week you should be able to step up to 6 feet away from your dog. You'll find it helpful to lay the leash on the ground stretched out in front of him. This way you can walk farther than the leash will allow, but if your dog moves you can simply pick up the leash as you tap the momentary button and reposition him. If at any time your dog should get up and move away from the place where you downed him, use a short leash grip to abruptly walk him back to the precise spot where you started, and down him there again until you release him.

As your dog becomes accustomed to your movement, begin to add duration back into the mix, but do not walk out of sight. When your dog is reliable at staying down calmly for 3 to 5 minutes when you are up to 10 feet away, you are ready for the next step.

ADDING DISTRACTIONS TO THE DOWN

It will be important that your dog learns to resist temptation when on a *down* command. Although you have prepared him to understand that the command may involve duration and distance, for some dogs, distraction is the hardest part. That's because certain distractions may awaken your dog's prey—which includes play—drive. These are powerful instincts we discussed in Chapter 4. We have saved distractions for last because adding duration and distance have already helped your dog understand his responsibility to hold the position. Now it's time for us to teach him that once you have initiated a down, he is to hold that position until you release him . . . almost no matter what.

We say *almost* because very rarely there may be some credible reason for a dog to abandon the down. We recall one instance when out of nowhere came a stupendous clap of thunder right over our heads, moments after we had downed a dog. He sprang to his feet in fear. Rather than correct him, we calmly moved him indoors and successfully completed the exercise. However, if you pick a safe and reasonable place for your dog to do the down, make sure you hold him accountable to stay until you release him.

Here is how you add distractions to the down:

1. Rather than seek a quiet area to do the down, select a place where moderate activity will be within your dog's line of sight, but at least 15 feet away. By moderate activity we mean people moving around, children playing, etc. Don't allow other pets or people close to your dog at this time, but do begin to vary locations.

2. You can create your own distraction to help proof the exercise by downing your dog on your left side while you hold a sock or dish towel in your right hand. At New Skete, we often use baseball caps because the trainers are usually wearing them. Hold the leash and remote control in your left hand, finger poised on the constant button.

3. Don't show the object to your dog or tease him with it, but toss the object several feet to your right, away from your dog.

4. The first few times you do this, repeat the word *down* and tap the momentary button at the same time you throw. We use the momentary button here because it is the quickest tap possible and is more likely to affirm to the dog he should stay down, compared to a tap of the constant button, which might, depending on the dog, make him feel like he should move.

5. If he gets up, swiftly grip the leash close to the training collar, place him exactly where he was, hold the constant button down on the educational level, say *down*, and apply quick downward leash pressure, all at the same time. Release the button the instant your dog downs.

6. Within a week your dog should be able to hold the down even if a squeaky toy is surreptitiously tossed 5 or 6 feet in front of him.

7. When your dog does resist temptations like this, you can reward him *while he is still holding the down* by placing a treat between his front paws.

With your dog in the down position, calmly place a toy on the ground

Repeat the command

Eventually, you'll release your dog to play with the toy

8. Release your dog fairly soon after he has shown that he will stay down despite a distraction. For the first few days, 20 to 30 seconds is long enough.

9. If you used a toy, after you release your dog, allow him to play with it.

When your dog has reliably held the down for 1 week with all the distractions you have encountered and set up, you can begin to add back duration. Then, when your dog will reliably stay down for 3 to 5 minutes with distractions, you can begin to add back distance in the way you originally taught it. Eventually your dog will understand the *down* command very well and will be able to do it without the leash.

One final note about distractions: be reasonable with your dog. We recall two clients who called us to complain that their dog would get up during a certain distraction. One client's 2-year-old child was crawling literally on top of the dog, throwing cereal in her face. The other client placed his dog in a down in the backyard and then used the lawn mower. "Darn dog gets up every time I get within 15 feet of him," he complained. Remember, do work to create a reliable down, but be reasonable and fair to your dog.

By now your walks should be pleasant and your dog's indoor behavior should have started to improve. Get ready, because an even bigger payoff is coming! We're about to introduce lessons that will lead directly to a reliable off-leash recall. And once your dog knows that, not only will many behavior problems diminish, but you'll have made her much safer.

You should be walking your dog *on a loose leash* a minimum of twice per day for 20 minutes each. You have instituted leash manners with the judicious use of training collar, leash, and e-collar. Although he may still need an occasional reminder, your dog understands that he is to walk by your side and that he is not to stop and sniff every bush nor lunge at every bird or squirrel he sees. And you have also integrated recalls and sits into the walks. Make provisions for your dog to potty at specific points during the walk. We recommend the beginning, middle, and end. During the training, do not allow your dog to stop constantly. However, if your dog clearly needs to go urgently, then of course you should allow that. These outdoor walks not only contribute to your dog's training but also help you spend time together, sharing mutual experiences. This structured time, combined with these togetherness adventures, will continue to build the relationship.

In most cases, a happy by-product of the lesson plan up to this point is improved behavior in a general sense. We have not yet trained for specific problem behaviors such as excessive barking, counter surfing, or jumping. (Soon we will, but we have a few important skills to teach first.) Yet at this point in a dog's training program, many of our clients report that their dogs not only respond to the specific lessons they are being taught but that problem behaviors begin to diminish even though they were not yet directly addressed. We believe there are several reasons this is a common experience.

First, much of naughty dog behavior is fueled by boredom and frustration. Dogs are energetic, intelligent beings. If their physical and psychological needs for stimulation are not met by their Pack Leader, the dog must find some outlet for all that energy. In other words, if you don't give your dog a job, he'll write his own job description . . . and you probably won't like it. By walking your dog and training him for a few minutes several times a day, you are giving him exercise for the body as well as new challenges for the brain. Both are good because they give your dog a job on which to focus.

Second, the mere act of spending quality time with your dog is enormously beneficial to the overall relationship. Before you embarked on this new training adventure with your dog, you may have played with him sometimes and walked him others. But did you *really* focus on him as deeply as you have recently? It's easy enough to toss the ball for your dog with one hand and play with your phone in the other. But that means your dog only gets part of your attention, and believe us when we tell you that dogs know the difference. When you are truly engaged with your dog in a productive way, you have an opportunity to mind meld with him that you cannot achieve any other way. Better leash manners allow you to take your dog with you to more places. A reliable sit is useful when checking into or out of the vet, and it comes in very handy if you bring your dog into a store that allows pets. A well-taught down

Pointing as you down your dog eventually becomes a hand signal your dog will recognize and obey

means that your dog won't have to be locked up when guests who may be nervous about dogs come for a visit.

Third, we humans are a confusing species. Thankfully, dogs find us as loveable as we find them. But much of the time we do not do a good job of making household rules clear to our dogs. When they are puppies, we pick them up and encourage them into our laps. We may even want to cuddle with them at convenient moments when they are older and larger. But how is the dog to know when we want them climbing on us and when we don't? We get excited to see the dog, so the dog jumps. And then we scold. Not only do we scold, but people often reprimand with a torrent of angry words in a language that dogs simply do not understand. Your training plan has brought some welcome *clarity* into your relationship so that your dog not only begins to understand *what* you want, but he also learns to care about pleasing you. That's a clear sign that you are becoming a good Pack Leader.

Preparing for Good Behavior Off Leash

Since we have established good manners on leash, your dog has learned to pay more attention to *you* and less to environmental distractions. That is a game changer when it comes to taking pleasant neighborhood walks. Yet many people will want to go a step further and train their dog to be responsive when off leash in such areas as dog parks or other large, open spaces where dogs are permitted off leash. You can benefit from off-leash control of your dog even if you live in the suburbs and want to help your dog be safer in your yard. And that brings us to a quick word of warning about safety. It is your responsibility to make good decisions for your dog. Although we encourage you to teach off-leash obedience, and although we will help you achieve it, please be mindful of basic safety and of the leash laws in your community. A backyard is a wonderful place for your dog to enjoy, but don't leave even trained dogs unattended in the yard. Too many things can go wrong in your absence. And just because you eventually *can* walk your dog off leash in busy areas doesn't mean you *should*. Safety first.

We remember riding in a taxi on a traffic-filled Manhattan street. Midtown was hopping that day. The streets were filled with cars and trucks and honking, Vehicles trying to pass. Bicycles weaving in and out. Pedestrians forging into intersections, trying to cross en masse. While stopped at a red light, we noticed a man walking with a beautiful Doberman at his side. The dog was heeling perfectly. The man was walking purposefully and with obvious pride in the fact that in the middle of New York City, during rush hour, *his dog was completely off leash*. He wasn't even carrying a leash in his hand. Our first thought was to admire the dog's obviously excellent training. Our second thought was less sanguine. We remember thinking, "Mister, one mistake, one unexpected distraction in this traffic and your dog is dead." So remember, *yes,* we are going to teach your dog good off-leash manners that you will both enjoy. But safety first!

Preparing for Off-Leash Purposeful Walking

Approximate time: 15 minutes

How many times to repeat this lesson per day: 2

How many days to repeat this lesson: 5, but do not progress beyond this lesson until your dog is performing it reliably.

Equipment: A 15-foot long line attached to the training collar of your choice. The e-collar will be on the dog, and the remote control will be in whichever hand is not holding the long line. Keep a finger ready on the constant button. Have treats in your pocket.

Purpose of the lesson: ❶ To teach your dog to follow you when off leash; ❷ to teach your dog to come when you call off leash; ❸ to teach your dog to sit off leash.

Location: Ideally, we begin in a large area where major distractions are somewhat reduced. If you live in the city with limited open space access, you may wish to start in a long hallway of your apartment building. Eventually you can work your way up to a dog park. Or you can start there if you teach this lesson when other dogs are not present. In the suburbs or country, a large backyard or field will do nicely, provided there aren't other dogs running loose. It is important for you to vary your lesson locations so your dog learns to respond to you in new and different areas.

How to select a level: Start on your dog's normal educational level, the one that most often worked in Lesson 8 outside your home. You may need to lower or increase the level depending on your dog's response. But don't be surprised if you need to raise the level slightly, given that you are going to allow the dog to get farther from you in a new environment. As always, reduce the level if your dog shows a worried reaction, and increase it if he seems not to feel it. Be aware that levels tend to rise and fall more frequently when you are training outdoors than they do indoors. That's because distractions outdoors are constantly changing.

If your dog gets tangled in the line: As you progress and let out more line, your dog will quickly learn to step over or through it without becoming tangled. But at first even a small tangle may concern some dogs. If your dog stops moving because he thinks he is tangled—and you observe that he could easily free himself just by walking through it—move ahead a few feet and verbally encourage your dog to come to you. Once he's moving, resume your Purposeful Walk. Go back to untangle your dog only if he has really hogtied himself in the line.

A few words of caution: As you feed out more and more long line, you will find your dog moving ahead of you, perhaps falling a bit behind you if something catches his interest and changing sides from left to right. All of this is permitted provided he checks in with you and does not tighten the leash. Remember, this lesson does not teach the dog to heel down a crowded city street. It teaches him to stick with you the way you would need him to when he is off leash and you are going for a hike or playing in the park. Watch your feet and do not get tangled in or trip on the long line. You may need to switch the long line and/or remote control from one hand to the other from time to time. Unless you have a very small dog, when you need to switch hands, don't pass the long line from hand to hand behind your back, even if that seems quicker. If your dog spots a distraction and runs, your shoulder could get pulled. When you are recalling your dog, you may be walking backward. Be aware of what is behind you so that you don't fall.

Note: Over time, your dog learns the lesson and becomes reliable at walking in your vicinity, changing directions when you ask and coming to you when called. At least the first few minutes of each lesson should look very much like any Purposeful Walk you have previously done. That helps your dog focus on you as the Pack Leader. But eventually this lesson will begin to resemble a walk or frolic in the park much more than it appears to be a formal training session.

Moreover, that is the goal because it will be fun for both of you. However, be aware of training opportunities such as when your dog will have to decide whether to remain with you or run off and chase a squirrel. Stay aware of your surroundings and, ideally, call your dog to you for a reward before he flips into prey drive rather than after.

Lessons to prepare for off-leash Purposeful Walks consist of several key components:

Let's go. This is what we say when we change directions and ask the dog to turn around and follow us.

Recall. If the dog gets too far ahead of us, we say her name and *come* when we want her to reverse directions and come right to our feet, where we ask her to sit and wait. This is what we taught the dog starting with Lesson 7. Dog trainers call this a recall. (You can also call your dog to you if he is substantially behind you, in which case you would turn *toward* your dog and ask for the recall.)

Pause to rest. When we stop walking to take a moment of rest, we teach the dog to remain relatively close to us. During this break, we don't usually care if the dog is standing, sitting, or lying down. We let him pick. The pause helps both you and your dog take a moment to collect your thoughts.

Check-ins. As your dog begins to absorb this lesson, you will notice him looking at you more. Some dogs make brief full eye contact. Others use their peripheral vision to look at you. In either case, the dog is making sure that his behavior aligns with what you are asking. Therefore, we want to quietly acknowledge the check-in with a calm word of praise. We tend to say *yes* or *hi* as the dog looks at us. This confirms for the dog that he is doing the right thing, and we find it encourages him to continue and even try harder.

We will start with the *let's go* command. This builds on what you taught in Lessons 2 and 4, when you taught your dog to walk politely on leash by your side.

The difference here is that, as the lesson progresses, we will begin to feed out more leash than we did in those prior lessons. Here is how we begin.

1. Start with the dog on your left. Bundle the long line up in your left hand so that the dog feels a loose leash with only a foot of slack. If the line is too bulky to hold in a bundle, you can toss most of it on the ground behind you and hold only a small section of the line between you and the dog. Hold the remote in your right hand, finger poised on the constant button.

2. Pick two objects, such as specific trees or fence posts that are on opposite sides of your training space and are as far apart as possible. Let's call them targets 1 and 2. You'll need to periodically glance at them as you walk—heading right for one or the other—so you don't wind up walking in circles. Pack Leaders know where they are going, and your dog will respond far better if you move purposefully rather than aimlessly.

3. Say *let's go* and step out *briskly* toward target 1 with shoulders back, chin up, and eyes forward because this is a Purposeful Walk. If your dog begins to tighten up the leash by pulling ahead of you, tap the constant button and swiftly execute a right about-turn. Now you are walking back toward target 2. Five or six steps later, turn again and walk toward target 1. Your ultimate goal is to walk with your dog all the way to the first target, to take a moment of rest there, and then to walk with your dog all the way back to the second target. Imagine that you want to teach your dog to do this, staying relatively close to you *even when there is no leash.*

4. Rather than run ahead of you, your dog may also stop to sniff something enticing. If it is obvious he has to eliminate, stop and permit that. However, *we do not stop if the smell is simply a*

distraction. If your dog stops to sniff, he might be so distracted that he doesn't notice that you are walking farther and farther away from him. In this case, *keep going* but tap either the constant or vibration button an instant *before* the long line gets tight. Keep walking but encourage your dog to catch up to you by saying *let's go*. Once he catches up, mark any check-in with a *good* or *yes*.

5. If this training space is new to your dog, you'll find him a little more distracted than usual. But because the exercise starts exactly like leash lessons he has done many times before, you should quickly find him calming down and walking at your side without tightening the long line.

6. As your dog commits to maintaining a loose leash walk with you, feed out a foot of leash so that if your dog wants to move a bit ahead of you he can do that. For the first time in his training, you will permit him to get ahead of you, but you will not permit him to tighten the long line. Gauge his speed and attention level to note when the leash is about to be pulled tight. Before the leash tightens, tap, say *let's go*, and execute a swift about-turn back toward the other target.

7. Eventually you should be able to walk all the way to one of the targets. Praise any check-ins along the way. When you get to the target, stand still for a moment of rest. Your dog can stand, sit, or lie down at his own discretion. He can sniff. He can roll a bit. However, if he becomes highly distracted (or if he has rested quietly for a few minutes), resume the Purposeful Walk by saying *let's go*, and head back to the other target. If your dog looks at you when you say *let's go*, do not tap the button. If he does not look at you, tap the constant button as you take your first step. Continue to your other target, turning only if you need to remind your dog not to tighten the long line.

(8) During this 15-minute session, you will be turning your dog back between targets multiple times. Do it with your Purposeful Walk body language because this helps remind the dog to remain close enough to you that he does not tighten the leash. However, you can accomplish the same goal by asking your dog to *come* when called, just as you did in Lesson 8. If your dog should become distracted and begin to walk so far ahead of you that he is surely going to tighten the leash, tap the button, say your dog's name paired with *come*, and switch directions from walking forward to backward. As you walk backward, hold out your hand as you have always done with a treat, draw your dog into your space, and ask for the sit with the upward motion of your hand. Once he sits in front of you, say *Yes!* then give him a treat when he is in the sitting position. If your dog doesn't easily apply the *come* command in this context, put pressure on the long line to initiate the dog's movement toward you and induce him to sit in front of you at your feet. If you have to help him frequently with the line over the next few days, that is a sign that you need to go back and practice Lesson 8 more and with more distractions.

In upcoming sessions you should be able to feed out a foot or two of long line per day and maintain the same schedule of walking between your targets. Your dog can use most of the long line that you feed out, but if he tries to use all of it, he will tighten the leash. When you deduce that is about to happen, do one of the following:

- Reverse direction, tap, and call your dog to sit in front of you, complete with hand motion/treat, which has become a hand signal.

- Tap and say *let's go* as you turn back to your other target.

Every day begin your session by giving only a foot of slack in the leash to the dog. But a few minutes into your lesson, let out a foot or two more line than you did the

Your dog may move substantially ahead of you

Reverse direction and call your dog to you

day before. Keep the progression going until eventually you can purposefully walk your dog holding only the handle at the end of your line.

You are ready to go to the next lesson when:

- You are consistently able to hold the end of a long line that is at least 15 feet long and walk your dog through a big space without your dog tightening up the line.

- Your dog usually notices your turns and follows you with *no* command. Or, if he's distracted, you can easily get him to follow you when you tap, turn, and say *let's go*.

- Your dog consistently comes when called and sits in front of you, even when he is nearly at the end of the long line. You no longer have to reel the line in to get him to come or sit, even in the presence of minor distractions in the environment.

Brother Christopher backs away from the dog, hand outstretched, drawing the dog into his space. Sometimes, but not always, the hand conceals a treat.

Using a long lead, start walking your dog

Occasionally reverse and call your dog to you to keep him engaged

How to Advance the Off-Leash Purposeful Walk

Approximate time: 15 minutes

How many times to repeat this lesson per day: 2

How many days to repeat this lesson: 5, but do not progress beyond this lesson until your dog is performing it reliably.

Equipment: A 15-foot long line attached to the training collar of your choice, and a 20-foot (or longer if needed) length of parachute cord onto which you have secured a bolt snap so you can attach it to your dog's training collar. The e-collar will be on the dog, and the remote control will be in whichever hand is not holding the long line. Keep a finger ready on the constant button.

Purpose of the lesson: ❶ To teach your dog to turn around and follow you when farther than 15 feet from you; ❷ to teach your dog to come when you call off leash even if your dog is farther than 15 feet from you and even if there are distractions.

Location: By now you have practiced Purposeful Walking on a long line in various places. Start this lesson in one of the locations with which your dog is most familiar. If you have the option, begin in a large fenced space. Eventually, practice this lesson in all of your previous locations. Then you can go to new places, assuming your dog earns your confidence with his responsiveness when you call him to pack up.

How to select a level: Start at your dog's most frequently used level from the prior lesson. However, do be ready to turn it up or down as necessary according to his reaction or lack of reaction. Be prepared, because this lesson will involve a new challenge.

When your dog is focused on you, drop the line . . .   *. . . and move purposefully forward*

> **Note:** Tie knots every few feet in the parachute cord in the event you need to step on it to stop your dog from running away. The knots will stop the cord from slipping under your foot. The parachute cord is used as an insurance policy because your dog is new to off-leash freedom. You cannot pick up parachute cord when the dog is running because it will burn your hands. Instead, you can step on it if you need to stop him. It is light and will give your dog the sense that he is not on a leash.

Begin this lesson by holding only the end of the 15-foot long line, saying *let's go* and turning as needed to ensure your dog does not hit the end of the line. Occasionally call your dog to you, reverse to walk backward, and hold out your hand with or without a treat. The outstretched hand has become his hand signal to come to you.

Your dog should be walking within 15 feet of you on a loose line, checking in with you once in a while, and responding easily to your *let's go* command for turns and when you call him to sit in front of you. Give your commands without tapping the button, but if you have to repeat the command a second time, tap the constant button as you repeat the command, especially if he is preoccupied with scents on the ground. If that doesn't work, then either you need to go back and practice previous lessons more, or you need to turn up the e-collar slightly due to a higher distraction level.

Within a few minutes of starting this lesson, you should feel that your dog is plugged into you. By this we mean that he is connected to you psychologically. He demonstrates this connection by visually checking in with you, by running and even playing but redirecting himself to stay with you when you begin to move farther away from him but *before the leash tightens*. Once you attain this level of attention and control, here is what you do next:

1. Start with your dog very close to you.

2. While you are Purposefully Walking, drop the long line and let it trail behind your dog on the ground.

3. Pick up your pace so that, as Pack Leader, you appear even more purposeful than before. Chin up, shoulders back, eyes forward.

4. Focus on a location target and head for it briskly.

5. Walk forward for about 10 feet—assuming your dog stays within a few feet of you—then tap the constant button as you say *let's go* and turn around. Walk the 10 feet back to about where you started, and again tap the constant button as you say *let's go* and turn around. This puts your dog on notice that he is to remain focused on you. (Note that if he didn't stay within a few feet of you for those first 10 feet, you should pick up the line and decide whether he is really ready for you to drop it. If at any point you believe your dog is about to run away from you, step on the line, pick it up, and repeat Lesson 10 for another few days.)

6. From this point, if your dog stays close to you, go all the way to your target, ask your dog to sit, give him a treat, and take a moment of rest. If your dog wishes to lie down or roll, this is a good time to permit that, provided he does not leave your vicinity.

7. Your dog may want to run and play while you are walking. You can permit that, provided he remains within 15 feet of you.

8. Occasionally call your dog by telling him to come and asking him to sit. A particularly opportune moment to do this is if your dog should decide to move farther than 15 feet from you.

9. Practice sits or downs for 2 or 3 minutes once or twice during your Purposeful Walk.

Ask your dog for eye contact

If your dog becomes distracted, tap the button, walk backward, and call him to you

How to Finalize the Off-Leash Purposeful Walk

Approximate time: 15 minutes

How many times to repeat this lesson per day: 2

How many days to repeat this lesson: 10 days minimum

Equipment: Parachute cord. You will also attach the 15-foot long line you have been using to the training collar of your choice. Yes, for the moment your dog will have two lines attached to his training collar. Be careful your feet don't get tangled in the lines. The e-collar will be on the dog, and the remote control will be in whichever hand is not holding the long line. Keep a finger ready on the constant button. Have treats in your pocket.

Purpose of the lesson: To teach your dog to obey all the same commands you have taught and practiced previously but in a scenario where the dog feels more freedom of choice.

Location: The first few times you teach this lesson, use a space you have worked in before, ideally at a time when distractions will be mild to moderate rather than high. If you have the option, begin in a large fenced space. As you progress, train in new and more distracting environments.

How to select a level: Start at your dog's most frequently used level from the prior lesson. However, be ready to turn it up or down as necessary according to his reaction or lack of reaction. Be prepared because this lesson will involve a new challenge.

For the first 5 minutes, conduct this lesson holding the end of the 15-foot long line. The parachute cord is also attached to the training collar but is dragging behind the dog.

1. During these 5 minutes, turn your dog several times and call him at least twice to ensure that he is paying attention and is willing to stay close to you when you turn or pack him up to sit in front of you.

2. Provided your dog shows willingness to remain close during the start of the Purposeful Walk, recall your dog to sit in front of you.

3. Give a treat while he is in the sitting position and remove the long line. Put it in your pocket in case you need it later in the lesson. Leave the knotted parachute cord attached to his training collar and dragging behind him.

4. Quickly resume the Purposeful Walk, throwing in turns as you say *let's go*. Your goal is similar to that of the previous lesson: to walk from one end of your training space to the other, your dog turning when you ask him to and coming to you when you call.

Your dog does not have to remain right by your side. And as in previous Purposeful Walk lessons using a long line, he may switch from your left side to your right. He may move ahead or linger a bit behind. However, do keep your dog within reach of the parachute cord so that you can step on it if he becomes distracted to the point where you believe he may run away. At any point you can snap the long line back on the training collar, especially if you need to actually hold the end of it in your hand for safety purposes. Never hold the parachute cord because it will burn your hands if the dog runs.

Use the e-collar as needed if your dog becomes distracted to the point where you have to repeat a command. Be alert to distractions 360 degrees around you. Anticipate what your dog might do even before he does it. For example, if you see someone walking a dog in the distance before your dog notices, be prepared to turn him or call him away from that distraction before or the instant he sees it, rather than after. Once you have practiced this lesson in multiple places over the course of 1 week, consider whether you have had to step on the parachute cord to stop your

Once your dog has experience, place him on a sit stay

Call your dog to you from a distance

dog. If you have not had to physically intervene, and instead you have simply used your voice, your e-collar and your Purposeful Walking body language to maintain confident control, then you are ready to cut 2 feet off the end of your parachute cord. Don't be tempted to just eliminate the line altogether. Instead, every few days cut off another foot or two.

Even when you and your dog are in harmony, only practice the off-leash Purposeful Walk in locations where it is *legal and safe* to have a dog off leash. Although we are professional dog trainers, we don't practice off-leash training near traffic. Yes, we are confident that we can call back a distracted dog who has taken off after something, but we know from experience it will take us a moment to tap the button on an effective level and call the dog. It takes another moment for the dog to turn around to come back to us. If you have practiced sufficiently, *the training will work*. This is the benefit of having practiced all those *let's go* commands in your home and on your outdoor Purposeful Walks. You need distance from danger to give yourself and your dog time to respond to one another.

Think back to the Pack Leader of the African wild dogs. She marches her pack right through the midst of myriad distractions, but her pack remains close to her, following her lead. This is who you have become to your dog. Naturally your dog may need a reminder from time to time, so you should be prepared to practice any of these lessons as your dog may require.

Go to Place

Approximate time: Varies from 5 to 15 minutes, depending on the day

How many times to repeat this lesson per day: 2 or 3

How many days to repeat this lesson: 10 days minimum

Equipment: A dog bed as described in the lesson, and a 6-foot leash or 15-foot long line attached to the training collar of your choice. The e-collar will be on the dog, but you will not use it until Day 3 and after. Have treats handy.

Purpose of the lesson: To teach your dog to go to his place and remain there until released.

Location: Various; starting inside your home and eventually moving outside if you wish.

As you can see from our training schedule, we recommend starting this lesson after you complete Lesson 12; you'll teach it at the same time as you're teaching off-leash reliability. However, if the Place exercise is more important for your family's needs, you may want to start this lesson after you have completed Lesson 10. In either case, before we give specific instructions for this lesson, it is important for us to offer some preparatory information.

You're relaxing at home and the relative quiet is shattered by the doorbell, closely followed by hysterical barking and nails scrabbling on the floor. As you approach the door and reach for the knob, your dog continues barking. If he's friendly, he may begin jumping at the door in excited anticipation. "Guests! Visitors! New people to pet me!" If your dog does not prefer the company of strangers, he is also barking in excited anticipation but with different thoughts. "Invaders! Barbarians! New people to repel!" In either case the commonality is excessive excitement triggered by that doorbell. What if you could easily send your dog to a nearby dog bed? How convenient would it be for him to remain there in his place quietly for a reasonable length of time?

With Lesson 5 we taught your dog to sit at the door. This reduces overexcitement at that location for many dogs. And in Appendix: Dog Behavior Problems, we will discuss another solution for what we call "door frenzy" in case the issue is persistent. We suggest you read that strategy if you have this problem because it offers an approach that can later be combined with the *place* command. However, the Go to Place exercise itself will offer a solution to this common problem.

Preparing for the *Go to Place* Command

We recommend using a platform dog bed, which will become your dog's place. This is one that is raised a little off the ground on short legs. Although your dog can easily hop onto the bed, the fact that it is a very well-defined space makes this exercise easier for him to learn. It also makes it easier to resist the temptation to hop off the bed before you give him permission. We use a platform bed big enough for the dog to lie down and stretch out if he wishes. The bed will have a metal or PVC pipe frame with tear-resistant fabric stretched over it. Alternatively, you can use a thick-cushioned dog bed if you already have one. But use one that has raised bolstered cushions on three sides. Your dog can nestle into the bed, and he'll feel more contained than he would on a flat cushion or mat alone. Once your dog is very familiar with this command, you'll be able to transition him to a more portable place, such as a mat that you can roll up and bring with you anywhere.

Some dogs are curious and fearless about new surfaces. They are happy to jump on and explore anything new. Other dogs are very reluctant to tread a surface which they haven't experienced before. So if you are going to teach this command on a new bed, it's best to test your dog's willingness to hop onto it before you begin the lesson. Put your dog on a leash and gently attempt to guide him onto the bed. You can also show him you have a treat, and when you get him close to the bed, toss the treat onto it. If your dog shows zero reluctance about hopping onto the bed, you're ready to begin the first lesson. But if your dog is not sure about stepping onto something new, you might try covering the entire bed with a blanket or beach towel for the first few days. Dogs are familiar with those surfaces. You can try flipping the bed upside down so that all four little legs are sticking up in the air and the cloth material is on the ground. Now it will feel and look more stable. After a few days, you'll be able to turn it right side up. Or, finally, place a couple of high-value treats (think chicken) on the floor close to the bed, then over the next few days, on the very edge of the bed, and finally, you can start tossing the treats farther and farther toward the center of the bed. Use a leash to help guide your dog for this preparatory exercise, but don't force him.

What *Go to Place* Is For . . . and What It Is Not For

There are a few ideal uses for this command, such as our example of when visitors first arrive, if the pizza delivery person is afraid of dogs, or if you just broke a glass on the kitchen floor. You can point at a bed that is 10 or 15 feet away and ask your dog to go wait on his place. Five or six minutes later you can go to your dog, praise him, and then release him. By this time the pizza delivery person is gone or you have visitors for your dog to greet, but he should be over that initial rush of excitement.

The *go to place* command can also be part of a solution for dogs who are overly possessive of their owners. For example, if you have a dog who objects when your children or other pets want to be close to you, send that possessive dog to his bed when you want to share affection with the others. Give your dog a place to be and a job to do while you show him that you are not a dog toy to be guarded from other family members. We wrote extensively about how to use space as a resource in our book, *Let Dogs Be Dogs*. And while we suggest professional assistance if you are dealing with a serious aggression problem, teaching the *place* command is a good start. As a general rule, avoid petting, touching, or even talking to the dog while she is doing her job by remaining on her place. You've given her a job to do, so let her do it without undue interference.

Sometimes you'll only need your dog on that bed for 5 minutes to clean up a broken glass. Other times you might want him calming down on his bed for 15 minutes before greeting a guest. If you sit on a nearby sofa to read, you can keep your dog on his bed for longer than 15 minutes. Eventually you might want to work up to having your dog wait on her place while you eat a meal. But remain in sight of the bed so you can correct any attempt your dog might make to abandon ship. And as we had to advise one client having trouble making the *go to place* command work at home, be sure children aren't crawling all over the dog, throwing cereal on him!

Now that you're ready, we'll begin.

Go to Place Command: Days 1 and 2

1. Place your dog on your left side and hold the 6-foot leash in your left hand bundled up so that he only has 6 inches of slack. Walk him to the bed, guide him onto it with a forward motion of the leash, and say *go to place* just as your dog is stepping onto it.

2. When he is on the bed, create enough slack in the leash so that the dog does not feel tension unless he attempts to step off the bed. In that case, use just enough tension on the leash to intercept his movement, keeping him on the bed. Then create slack to remove tension on the leash. If your dog wishes to lie down on the bed, create enough slack in the leash to permit that.

3. Your dog may choose his own position on the place. We will allow him to stand, sit, or lie down. He will feel tension on the leash only when he is in the act of trying to get off. *This holds true through all lessons.*

4. Remain close to the bed, but don't hover over your dog.

5. You may have to intercept him a few times with the leash to stop your dog from getting off the bed. But when he commits to being there for a moment, you may give him a treat. Instead of giving it to

The leash is bundled up in your left hand so that the dog only has 6 inches of slack

Guide him onto the place with forward motion of the leash

Allow your dog to stand, sit, or lie down on the place

him by hand, drop the treat on the bed. Eventually, this approach will make going to place a reward unto itself.

6. Do not allow your dog to get a foot off the bed until you release him. Release him by saying his name and *let's go*. Then walk your dog off the bed, holding the leash. Take a 1-minute break, then repeat until you have done this three times. The entire lesson will only take about 5 minutes. Repeat the lesson three times daily at different times of day.

Note: Naturally you will need to glance at your dog to see what he is doing, but don't lock eyes with him. Use peripheral vision or glance only briefly. Turn slightly away from your dog so that your side is facing him rather than your front. Your body language makes it clear to the dog that you want him to remain in place. *This concept holds true through the entire set of lessons for this command.*

Go to Place Command: Days 3 and 4

1. Put your dog on a 6-foot leash. Walk him to the bed, say *go to place*, and toss a treat on it *just as he begins* to step onto the place. At this stage, your dog should get on the bed of his own volition, but if he does not, use the leash to gently but insistently propel him forward.

2. Once he is on the bed, create enough slack in the leash so that he does not feel any tension. However, use the leash to intercept and prevent any attempt he may make to step off the bed.

3. If your dog attempts to get off the bed, tap the constant button at the exact same time you use the leash to check your dog from getting off. Use the educational level, a low level, one that your dog does not find upsetting but one you believe he feels.

4　Turn slightly sideways in relation to your dog, observe him, but don't lock eyes. Create slack in the leash so it does not become tight as you sidestep a foot or two from the bed.

5　Keep your dog on the bed between 3 and 5 minutes, during which time you will not talk to him.

6　Step back to your dog and release him by saying his name and *let's go*. Then walk your dog off the place, holding the leash.

Go to Place Command: Days 5 and 6

1　Use the 15-foot long line, but hold it close to your dog. Walk briskly toward the bed and—without stopping—when you are 3 feet away, toss a treat onto it and say *go to place*.

2　Your dog will want to move ahead of you to jump on the place and eat the treat, *so be sure to relax your grip on the leash*. Allow the leash to run through your fingers so that your dog can get onto the bed without feeling any tension on his training collar. (If your dog stops to remain by your side, use the line to gently but insistently propel him forward all the way onto the bed.)

3　You will remain approximately 3 feet away. Turn sideways in relation to your dog and use only *peripheral vision* to keep track of his position. Do not lock eyes with your dog lest he think you want him to come to you.

4　At this stage we want the dog to start making his own decisions. So if you see him debating whether or not to step off the bed, *do nothing*. Just wait. If he does try to step off the bed, tap the constant button at the education level *just as the first foot touches the floor*. If he does not fix it himself, step in and use the leash to place him back on the bed immediately.

5 If your dog tries to get off the bed repeatedly, evaluate whether you have really practiced the prior lessons as directed. If not, go back a step. If so, then turn the collar up slightly to reinforcement level.

6 Keep your dog on the bed between 3 and 5 minutes during which you will remain at least 3 feet away from the place unless you have to step closer while tapping the button to help him back onto the bed.

7 You should be able to walk a few steps in any direction so that your dog learns that you may move but that he should remain on the place. Let the long line out and take it in as needed. *Be careful not to put any tension on your dog's training collar.* Remember to stay sideways to your dog and avoid direct eye contact. This helps your dog understand you want him to remain in place.

8 Release the dog by walking back to the bed, pausing a moment, then saying his name and *let's go*. Walk the dog off the bed, holding the leash.

- -

Dogs Can Make Us Smile During Training

Our friend Mary was teaching the *go to place* command to a very smart labradoodle who quickly learned it. But Bella was determined to test the rules. At this stage in the training, Bella, while remaining on the place, touched her front right foot to the ground. Mary tapped the constant button using Bella's educational level. The dog looked like she was thinking for a moment. Then she quite deliberately touched her front left foot on the ground. Mary tapped the button. After just another moment, Bella (and Mary) repeated that sequence with each of her back feet. Bella paused for a good long moment, but Mary swears she could see the gears turning in Bella's head. And that's when Bella touched her nose on the ground. Mary smiled to herself at the dog's ingenuity as she tapped the button. And that's when Bella simply lay down on the place, now convinced that she really did have to do the exercise. Mary calmly praised her and placed a treat right between Bella's front feet as she lay down.

- -

Go to Place Command: Days 7 and 8

1. Put a treat on the empty bed when your dog is not looking, and eventually make this random. Sometimes a treat will be there, sometimes not. Random treats are more rewarding for your dog than a constant flow.

2. Put a 15-foot long line on your dog, holding it close to him. Walk your dog *very briskly* toward the bed, and *while you are still in motion* but 4 or 5 feet away from the bed, point to it and give the command. Release tension on the line as your dog runs to the bed. *Do not hold him back.*

3. Turn sideways to your dog and remain 5 or 6 feet away from the bed. Drop the long line on the floor.

4. Walk a few steps in various directions around the bed. Use peripheral vision to stay aware of any movement. By now, either your dog isn't trying to get off the bed or, if he is, he corrects himself when he feels a tap. If not, move quickly but unemotionally back to your dog and use the leash to guide him swiftly back onto the bed. Do not move on to the next step until your dog succeeds at this lesson for at least 2 days.

5. Release your dog by walking back to the bed, picking up the long line, pausing a moment, then saying his name and *let's go*. Walk him off the bed, holding the line.

Go to Place Command: Days 9 and 10

1. Place the 15-foot long line on your dog and allow it to drag on the floor. Encourage your dog to walk with you toward the bed. When

you are 8 or 9 feet away, point at the bed and say *go to place*. He should run and hop on the bed.

2. If your dog runs toward the place before you say the command, that's good. Just say *place* as he is stepping up onto it. Now that you have given the command, you can reinforce it and require him to stay there.

3. Without locking eyes with your dog, walk near the bed, toss a treat near his feet, then walk 8 or 9 feet away.

4. Use peripheral vision to watch for any foot that touches the ground off the bed. Tap the constant button on the reinforcement level if necessary; your dog should then correct himself. If not, move quickly but unemotionally back and use the leash to guide him abruptly back onto the bed. Do not move on to the next step until your dog succeeds at this lesson for at least 2 days.

5. By now you should be able to walk around the room doing light chores or even read in a chair for a while in sight of your dog. Practice for up to 15 minutes at a time. Light distractions in the room are OK, but be fair to your dog. Don't vacuum next to him or let children throw toys nearby.

6. Release your dog by walking back to the bed, pausing a moment, then saying his name and *let's go*. Walk him off the bed, holding the long line.

7. Once your dog gets very reliable at this command, you can introduce stronger distractions. For example, start sending him to bed for a few moments when company comes. Make sure they ignore the dog while he is on the bed. Use the long line until your dog proves reliable for a few weeks with it. Then you can eliminate the line.

With practice, you can send your dog to the place from farther away

To make it more fun, you can hide a treat on the place

How to Proof the *Go to Place* Command and Make It Really Useful

- For best results, always go back to your dog and say his name and *let's go* when you are ready to release him. Don't call him off the bed from a distance.

- You can make this exercise even more fun for your dog by occasionally dropping a treat on the bed for him to discover when you're not practicing the command.

- Multiple daily short practice sessions are better than one long session.

- When your dog goes to the place of his own volition, he may get off whenever he chooses. The only time he must wait for you to release him is when you send him there.

- Your dog may choose inconvenient moments to show off his place routine, hoping to earn praise or a treat. *Never scold your dog for getting on the bed!* If for some reason you didn't want him on his place (for example, if you wanted to take him for a walk), just encourage him off it.

- If your dog is very wiggly, you may find it helpful to use the *place* command when you want to do things such as put on his training gear, clean his feet, examine his ears, clip his nails, or groom him.

- Add duration, distance, and distractions little by little to proof the *place* command and to help your dog be reliable.

- If you want to teach him to stay on the place for 5 to 10 minutes when guests arrive, practice that by using a long line on your dog and the e-collar. Practice only with guests who will ignore your dog while you practice. They can make direct eye contact, talk to him, or pet him after you release him.

- For convenience, you can have multiple beds to use as places in different locations, but practice each stage on all of them.

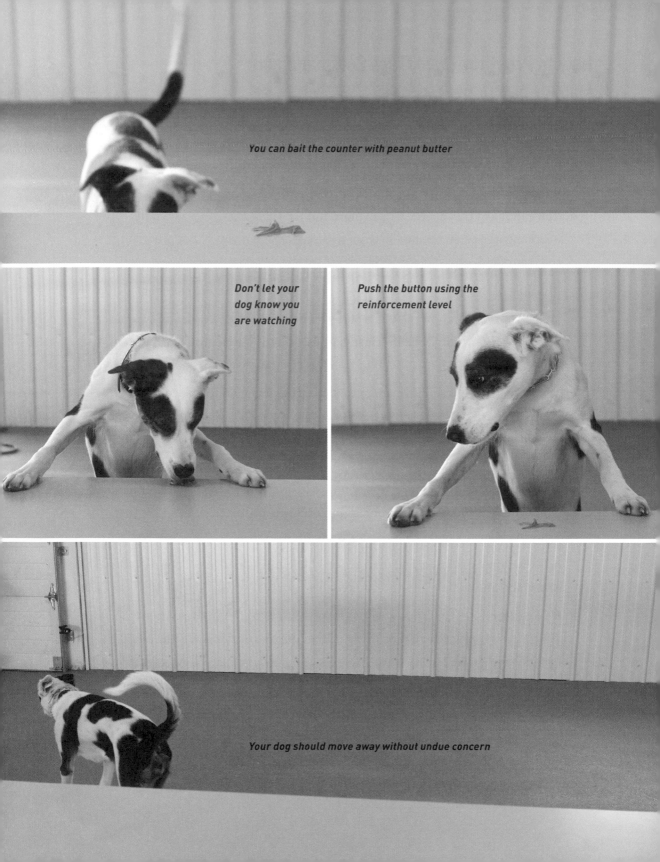

You can bait the counter with peanut butter

Don't let your dog know you are watching

Push the button using the reinforcement level

Your dog should move away without undue concern

The Silent Leave It

Approximate time: 5 minutes

How many times to repeat this lesson per day: 2 or 3

How many days to repeat this lesson: Until no longer needed.

Equipment: E-collar and your choice of a 6-foot leash or 15-foot long line, which you may eventually drop and later remove.

This solution helps to reduce or eliminate behaviors *which your dog should never do*. This is different from a behavior which you sometimes allow your dog to do, but not always. For example, your dog is *never* allowed to steal food from the counter. But sometimes you'll allow him to pick up and carry a stick he finds outside. Thus, you would use the silent version of the *leave it* command for counter surfing but not for picking up a stick at an inconvenient moment. We call this the "silent version" because you *say nothing* to the dog as you apply this problem-solving fix. You say nothing because ultimately you want your dog to avoid these areas or behaviors *even when you are not present* and when you are not shouting NO or otherwise warning him.

Here is how to teach the silent version of Leave It. We will use counter surfing as our example for these steps because that is one of the most common dog behavior problems reported to us. But this solution is useful for the variety of other problems we list below and in the appendix.

> **Note:** The e-collar will be on your dog before you start the next steps. At this stage, your dog is frequently wearing the e-collar anyway.

6   Use peripheral vision to observe. Be patient. Sooner or later your dog will notice the bait. Just wait. You may notice your dog seeming to think it over. "Should I or shouldn't I?" He may even look at you in this moment. Ignore him and do not let him know that you are aware. If and when the instant comes that your dog commits to doing the behavior, in this case making a very close sniff, lick, or even feet up on the counter, push the button, holding it down for no longer than one second. Say nothing. One of two things will happen:

- You have succeeded if your dog quickly stops the behavior. Better yet if he walks away from the area. In this case, you're done for the moment. But wait for 5 or 10 minutes before reducing observation and removing the bait.

- If you have pushed the constant button and your dog didn't even notice—and if he is continuing the behavior—then you may quickly increase the level and push the button again. *Remember, you can only push the button while your dog is actually doing the behavior, not after.*

7   Repeat twice per day for a week. If you are still able to catch your dog in the act, then you'll need to increase the level and start over. For about a week, be sure that your dog *does not have access to the problem area* unless you are prepared for the Silent Leave It. It is important that your dog not succeed in performing the problem behavior without interruption. You don't want your dog to randomly reinforce himself by occasionally scoring a cookie off the countertop. Remember, random reinforcement is very rewarding. If you are consistent, then he will find more profitable activities to do when unobserved, such as chewing his bone.

In addition to correcting the shenanigans of a counter-surfing dog, the Silent Leave It will correct many behavior problems, as described in the Appendix (page 257).

The Spoken Leave It means "not right now"

The Spoken Leave It

Approximate time: 5 minutes

How many times to repeat this lesson per day: 2 or 3

How many days to repeat this lesson: Until no longer needed.

Equipment: The e-collar and your choice of a 6-foot leash or 15-foot long line, which you may eventually drop and later remove.

Sometimes dogs find inconvenient moments to do a behavior which under different circumstances you would permit or even encourage. For example, you might teach your dog to fetch a stick in the yard. It's fun for both of you. But let's say that you're walking your dog down a crowded street and he spies a big stick on the ground. He wants to pick it up and carry it with him, which sounds cute. But let's say the stick is so big that it's going to knock into people passing by. What if it just looks really dirty? Or what if you're in a hurry and you simply don't have time to play the stick game? This is a good moment for you to use the Spoken Leave It. Another simple but valuable concept we'd like your dog to respect is the idea of "because I said so." For example, prey drive reactions will always make sense to your dog, but there are times you won't want to permit those . . . because you said so.

In the Appendix on page 257, we'll give details and notes on which problems lend themselves to the Spoken Leave It. The only difference from the Silent Leave It is that you'll say *leave it* as you push the button to interrupt the temporarily undesired behavior while redirecting your dog to something better. When you follow the instructions for the Silent Leave It, you're saying "not ever." But by speaking the words aloud, you're communicating "not now." That's why the Spoken Leave It is so valuable.

Now That You Have Completed the Lessons, Your Dog Knows a Lot!

You have taught all of these skills to your dog: leash manners, sit, sit at the door, down, off-leash walking with you, off-leash recall, and go to place. That's a lot! We encourage you to use this training every day in ways that will please not only you but also your dog. Remember, the relationship is about both of you. Dogs who are trained are enabled to reach their full potential. A trained dog can accompany you on more adventures than an untrained but well-loved dog. *Match love with training,* though, and you can do any of these activities with your dog:

- **Take daily leash walks** through the neighborhood during which your dog doesn't eat junk off the ground, doesn't lunge, and sits to politely greet admirers if he likes to be petted. Take at least two walks per day for a minimum of 20 minutes each to keep your dog exercised and mentally stimulated. (You started this with Lesson 2.)

- **Go to an outdoor café.** Here is the perfect venue to place your dog in a down (Lesson 10). But if you allow him up, you have taught him to stay near you without putting pressure on the leash (Lesson 1).

- **Play in the dog park** but come back when you call. Being able to recall your dog in the dog park is valuable, especially if he's near the gate when someone else is opening it (Lesson 7).

- **Spend more time with you and less in the crate.** When deliveries arrive, rather than your dog crowding or even sitting at the door, you can send him to

What this and so many more of the comments our clients make to us reflect is a connection that transcends obedience, what we at New Skete refer to as the spiritual dimension present in the human–dog relationship. The good news is that this isn't solely for monks. Our dogs help deepen our appreciation for the mystery of life, a mystery that is not confined to religion but is wide enough for any dog-loving person to experience. You may have started training your dog to solve problems like leash pulling or counter surfing, but beyond solving those specific problems, lessons such as Purposeful Walking, sit-stay, and the recall allow you and your dog to harmonize with life instead of feeling at odds with it.

We remember our dogs for our entire lives. We recall these relationships with a mixture of love and awe at the depth of those feelings . . . from both directions. Such feelings are why we humans continue to be so taken up with our canine friends. They have evolved from the hunters, guardians, and shepherds they started out to be into family. Our modern experience with dogs is far more positive and enriching than any problems we may have to navigate with them along the way. We hope this book has helped you unleash your dog's full potential—and your own!

We have tried to show you what you can achieve in your human–dog relationship, with a practical means to get there. The e-collar is not a silver bullet. It is simply a tool that, used with understanding and grace, can help you communicate clearly and safely with your dog. Such an enlightened relationship moves steadily toward a level of trust, devotion, and loyalty that transforms what is good into something great. When the relationship reaches this level, something magical is taking place.

Everyone wants to be able to let their dogs run off leash safely, and we hope that you have found that freedom through our program. We remember a conversation with a fellow trainer after she tried our method. She had been reluctant to use an e-collar, but afterward exclaimed, "You know what this feels like? It feels like freedom! I've never called my dogs off deer easier than now. And they seem quite happy about it as well."

We believe the method we have shared with you in this book will help you and your dog grow together in ways you might not even have imagined. We hope you will achieve a new level of freedom that both you and your dog will love.

LESSON PLANNER

DAY 1	**Lesson 1:** Introduce the Training Collar • Time/frequency: 5 minutes/2x day	NOTES & LEVELS: _____
DAY 2, 3, 4	**Lesson 2:** Introduce The Purposeful Walk with Training Collar • Time/frequency: 10 minutes/2x day **Lesson 3:** Teach Your Dog to Sit • Time/frequency: 2 minutes/4x day	NOTES & LEVELS: _____ _____ _____ _____
DAY 5, 6	**Lesson 4:** Introduce the Purposeful Walk with the E-Collar • Time/frequency: 10 minutes/2x day **Lesson 5:** Teach Your Dog to Sit at the Door • Time/frequency: 5 minutes/3x day	NOTES & LEVELS: _____ _____ _____ _____
DAY 7, 8, 9	**Lesson 5:** Teach Your Dog to Sit at the Door • Time/frequency: 5 minutes/3x day **Lesson 6:** Purposeful Walking with E-Collar and Outdoor Distractions • Time/frequency: 15 minutes/2x day **Lesson 7:** Introduce Coming When Called Inside the Home • Time/frequency: 3 minutes/3 to 5x day	NOTES & LEVELS: _____ _____ _____ _____ _____ _____
DAY 10, 11, 12	**Lesson 5:** Teach Your Dog to Sit at the Door • Time/frequency: 5 minutes/3x day **Lesson 6:** Purposeful Walking with E-Collar and Outdoor Distractions • Time/frequency: 15 minutes/2x day **Lesson 8:** Using Distractions to Build Reliability for the Indoor Call • Time/frequency: 5 minutes/3x day	NOTES & LEVELS: _____ _____ _____ _____ _____ _____

DAY 13, 14, 15

Lesson 5: Teach Your Dog to Sit at the Door
- Time/frequency: 5 minutes/3x day

Lesson 6: Purposeful Walking with E-Collar and Outdoor Distractions
- Time/frequency: 15 minutes/2x day

Lesson 9: Introduce Coming When Called Outside the Home
- Time/frequency: 3 minutes/2 to 4x day

NOTES & LEVELS:

DAY 16–22

Lesson 5: Teach Your Dog to Sit at the Door
- Time/frequency: 5 minutes/3x day

Lesson 6: Purposeful Walking with E-Collar and Outdoor Distractions
- Time/frequency: 15 minutes/2x day

Lesson 9: Introduce Coming When Called Outside the Home
- Time/frequency: 3 minutes/2 to 4x day

Lesson 10: Introduce the Down
- Time/frequency: 3 minutes/3 to 5x day

NOTES & LEVELS:

DAY 23–27

Lesson 5: Teach Your Dog to Sit at the Door
- Time/frequency: 5 minutes/3x day

Lesson 6: Purposeful Walking with E-Collar and Outdoor Distractions
- Time/frequency: 15 minutes/2x day

Lesson 11: Preparing for Off-Leash Purposeful Walking
- Time/frequency: 15 minutes/2x day

NOTES & LEVELS:

DAY 28–32

Lesson 5: Teach Your Dog to Sit at the Door
- Time/frequency: 5 minutes/3x day

Lesson 6: Purposeful Walking with E-Collar and Outdoor Distractions
- Time/frequency: 15 minutes/2x day

Lesson 12: How to Advance the Off-Leash Purposeful Walk
- Time/frequency: 15 minutes/2x day

NOTES & LEVELS:

Lesson 5: Teach Your Dog to Sit at the Door
- Time/frequency: 5 minutes/3x day

Lesson 6: Purposeful Walking with E-Collar and Outdoor Distractions
- Time/frequency: 15 minutes/2x day

Lesson 13: How to Finalize the Off-Leash Purposeful Walk
- Time/frequency: 15 minutes/2x day

Lesson 14: Go to Place
- Time/frequency: 5 to 15 minutes/2 or 3x day

NOTES & LEVELS:
_____
_____
_____
_____
_____
_____
_____
_____
_____
_____

APPENDIX: Dog Behavior Problems

In this appendix we will present solutions for over 40 dog behavior problems, many of which will be solved using techniques you and your dog have learned during the lesson plans outlined above. These are the issues that dog owners most frequently experience. Not only are many of these problems annoying, but some of them cause financial hardship when expensive personal property is destroyed. Remember the beagle who ate through the wall and then made confetti out of the couch? More troubling yet is that *tens of thousands* of dogs are injured when chewing inappropriately or doing other problem behaviors such as running away or chasing cars. And saddest of all, *hundreds of thousands* of dogs per year needlessly lose their homes when owners cannot resolve these issues.

But we can assure you that this cloud has a silver lining. The fact is that dogs are almost always willing to change their ways if only their humans could know exactly what to do. And when you read this appendix, you will know *exactly* what to do.

However, before we go on, it is imperative we repeat a point we stated earlier. ***Before you apply the solutions in this appendix, please train your dog per the lesson plans which precede it.*** We understand it is very tempting to skip right to this section, pick out the problems you're experiencing, and jump right to applying the corresponding solution. But we strongly request that you resist that temptation.

For you to enjoy an optimal relationship with your dog, it is critical for you to understand what actually causes dogs to engage in behaviors we can only describe as naughty, annoying, or downright dangerous. We have identified four root causes that drive most bad behaviors.

1. **Lack of clarity.** Many times a dog just can't understand what you're trying to say because you haven't explained it in a way that makes sense to his species. *We* are hardwired to talk and verbalize information to one another. *They*, however, usually use body language to communicate and explain concepts to one another and to us.

2. **Boredom.** We humans receive a lot of mental stimulation just commuting to work and getting through our day. We interact with family and friends all day through a smartphone linked to social media. But think of life from your dog's perspective. The only useful mental stimulation he gets is what you provide for him. A major benefit of regular Purposeful Walks is that it gives your dog a useful job to do and helps him feel fulfilled rather than bored.

3. **Frustration.** Dogs are complex problem-solving predators. They are domesticated, to be sure. But they have intellectual capacity that can too easily go unharnessed. If we don't provide an outlet for a dog's creativity, his needs remain perpetually unmet. He will become frustrated and invent his own outlets. Chances are, you won't like them.

4. **Genetics.** Collies will tend to nip at children's heels when they run. Labrador retrievers will want everything in their mouth. Huskies will enjoy digging in the yard. All of these are instinctual genetic tendencies we have cultivated in these breeds for good purpose. But if those tendencies are not channeled into useful jobs, the instinct remains but has nowhere to focus. That leads to problems.

Training your dog allows you to spend quality time with him, and causes you to create structured activities and a useful timetable for his day. That, combined with the clarity of purpose you achieve by training your dog, means that you will have addressed at least three of the four root causes of problem dog behaviors. If you train your dog following our instructions, chances are very, very good that he will have given up most of his problem behaviors before you ever get to apply the information in this appendix. At the very least, the intensity of these problems will have sharply decreased. And *that will make fixing them much easier for both of you.*

Many of the following dog behavior problems have similar solutions. Therefore, we have given you the Silent Leave It and the Spoken Leave It, both of which will work for various items on the problems list. Along with these procedures, we will identify which behaviors they correspond to so that you can apply the appropriate solution. Some of the problems have unique solutions, and we will detail those processes as well. In most cases, the e-collar allows us to impersonally and remotely interrupt behaviors we don't like. If we do that consistently, the dog will ultimately choose to stop those behaviors. The solutions below build on the training you have already done with your dog so that the e-collar will be effective at a far lower level than if you had not trained your dog.

Behaviors That Can Be Corrected Using the Silent Leave It

This solution helps to reduce or eliminate behaviors that your dog should never do. This is different from a behavior that you sometimes allow your dog to do, but not always.

Eats from the garbage can. Chances are the garbage can holds many happy memories for your dog. You might have to work on this one for a couple of weeks. During that time, when you cannot observe the can, lock it away.

Licks items in dishwasher. Remove knives when practicing.

Eats poop. You don't have to bait it. The poop is the bait, but clean up thoroughly when you cannot observe. If this is a persistent problem, consider upgrading your dog's food or consulting your veterinarian. For best hygiene, clean your yard daily.

Eats forbidden items such as rocks or goose/horse manure. Push the appropriate button *just as your dog's mouth makes contact* with the forbidden item.

Depending on the situation, you may need to do this while you're with your dog on a walk, from a distance while observing, or both.

Eats grass, dirt, mulch, or landscaping. Most veterinarians believe eating a blade or two of chemical-free grass won't hurt your dog, but some dogs want to ingest a lot of grass, mulch, or other landscape. Interrupt grass eating when you decide your dog should stop. For all other inappropriate materials, use the reinforcement level as soon as your dog shows intent to touch them with his mouth. Observation will be important for at least 2 weeks.

Scavenging on the walk. Just as your dog tries to pick up a forbidden object while on a leash walk, push the button, set to the educational level, *while in motion*. Walk briskly. Do not slow down or even break stride. After two or three walks, increase to the reinforcement level if necessary.

Eats out of cat litter box. Ideally you can move the litter (and cat food) to a location your cat approves but which your dog cannot access. In cases where this is not possible, use the Silent Leave It, but don't be surprised if you have to be extremely consistent for a long period of time.

Steals children's toys, laundry, cell phones, glasses, and other dogs' toys. Trying to steal another dog's toy can be dangerous, because it involves two problems: protectiveness and theft. Hit a reinforcement level proactively when the dog may even be thinking of taking the toy or object.

Chews destructively. Smear a little peanut butter on any furniture, wall, or molding the dog has previously chewed and use the Silent Leave It.

Digs holes in yard. You'll need an observation location where the dog cannot see you. Often a kitchen window works for this. You may need to bait a previously dug hole so the dog will want to dig there again when you're observing. If so, while he is not able to see you do it, pour water from a can of tuna or soup broth in the hole to attract the dog. Do not correct the dog for sniffing. Wait until the instant he begins to paw at the ground. Start with the educational level, but you may need to increase it to the reinforcement or interrupter level. You may also try vibration to interrupt the behavior. Observe every time the dog is in the yard for 2 weeks to catch and interrupt each instance. If digging continues, either you need to observe more carefully or you need to turn up the level at least slightly.

Runs fence or property line while barking at neighbors, dogs, or animals. Find an observation point as with "Digs holes in yard." Start by pushing the button on the educational level if your dog begins to obsess about distractions outside the yard. Increase to the reinforcement level if needed, but never chain or tie up your dog. To be fair to him, don't leave your dog outside alone for long periods of time, even in a fenced or electronically fenced yard, because this merely builds boredom and frustration. Bring your dog inside if neighbors or their dogs are deliberately provoking him.

Scratches at door to go out or come in. Some people don't mind this because they find it a useful signal. In other cases, the dog is damaging the door or clawing through a screen. In those cases, push the appropriate button just as your dog's paw makes contact with the door.

Fence jumping. This is a dangerous behavior and is tricky to correct because great consistency is required on your part for a few weeks. You'll need to carefully observe your dog in the yard behind the fence. You will notice that there is a point when the average dog will visually assess his distance from the fence to gauge the point from which he will jump. Some dogs will pace at this moment, others will be standing still. It can happen very fast, but the telltale sign for many dogs is when they look directly at the top of the fence to mark its height. The moment to push the button is that instant when the dog is gauging the fence to determine his jumping point. If the dog is climbing the fence, push the button when he first touches it. If the behavior persists, increase your vigilance, the level, or both.

Digs up carpet or picks at the threads. Start with the educational level rather than the reinforcement level because many dogs do this behavior when they are calm and more likely to feel a low level. We don't want to startle the dog. Instead, we want him to relax but find a more productive activity. After you push the button and the dog stops the behavior, give him a toy to chew instead.

Jumps on furniture he shouldn't. If your dog only gets on furniture when you are out of the room or out of the home, use computers or phones to set up a video observation point. You'll need to be consistent, so until you have resolved this issue, restrict your dog's furniture access to those times when you can observe and apply the Silent Leave It. The ideal moment to push the button is the instant your dog is about to jump, rather than after.

Marking in the house. Marking is different than elimination. This solution is only for marking, which is defined as repeatedly sprinkling a few drops to leave a scent on curtains, furniture, walls, or other objects, sometimes including people. This is an instinctual and often ingrained problem, so be patient and take 1 or 2 months to work on this problem. *Crate your dog when you cannot observe him.* When observing your dog, push the button on the reinforcement level *just as your dog lines up to hike his leg on an object.* For some but not all dogs, the vibration button will work well. If you interrupt and lightly penalize 100 percent of the next 100 attempts to mark, chances are you will solve this problem. If you catch a lower percentage, your chances of resolving the issue "markedly" decrease.

Mounts/humps people or dogs. This is a behavior which can cause a fight between two dogs, so we recommend you nip it in the bud by pushing the button on the educational level just as your dog expresses intent to hump. If the educational level doesn't work at first, try holding down the constant button for up to two seconds. If that doesn't work, try vibration, and if that doesn't work, go back to constant on the reinforcement level. Although we want to stop humping, we do want your dog to feel free to socialize with people and dogs. Therefore, don't rush. Find the lowest effective level and don't be surprised if it goes lower over time. If you are consistent, humping will stop altogether.

Behaviors That Can Be Corrected Using the Spoken Leave It

The Spoken Leave It is used when don't want your dog to do something at that moment. The Silent Leave It is for behaviors you don't ever want your dog to do. By saying *leave it*, you're communicating, "not now." That's why the Spoken Leave It is so valuable.

Begging for food. We're all for it if you want to give your dog healthy table scraps as a small percentage of his diet. But in many cases you can reduce or eliminate begging by mixing scraps only into his bowl of dog food and only at regular mealtimes. Feeding by hand, especially at the table, just sends the wrong message and creates the behavior. If, after 2 weeks, this new policy hasn't stopped your dog from begging, continue using it but in addition, when your dog begs at the table, push the button using the educational level, say *leave it*, then immediately send your dog to a nearby bed. Reinforce the *go to place* command as you learned in Lesson 14. Go to your dog, release him from the bed in 10 minutes, and repeat as necessary until the begging stops.

Nuisance barking/whining. Dogs will bark. It comes with the species, but excessive barking or whining is disturbing. Be sure you are not unduly confining your dog or failing to provide adequate exercise and leash walks. Boredom and frustration are the main causes of excessive barking. Assuming you are giving your dog the time and activity he needs, once he has exceeded reasonable amounts of noise, push vibration or the button on the reinforcement level as you say *leave it*. If necessary, you can even do this for dogs who bark when in the crate, although we do not recommend your dog wear the e-collar all night. Whining can be more difficult to correct because some dogs do it unconsciously, but a few well-timed taps of the button—along with *leave it*—can make them aware of it. In extreme cases, a bark collar will be more helpful than an e-collar. With the e-collar, you must be present to push the button. A bark collar automates the process and with its better timing may help the dog understand more quickly. When introducing a bark collar, always start on the lowest level and allow at least a full day before moving up a level. Give your dog time to learn at a reasonable pace, and chances are high you'll be able to avoid using a level that truly upsets your dog. When we have needed to use bark collars, we have had good results using those made by E-Collar Technologies, Dogtra, and Garmin. Each of them features low introductory levels that will not hurt the dog. However, we do not recommend using the automatic level increase function on any bark collar because we find the levels increase too quickly for some dogs to understand.

Barks at animals or people out of the windows. You may find it easier to practice if you place your dog on a leash and training collar so you can physically walk him away from the windows as you do the procedure. Be observant so you can catch your dog just as he is about to overreact at animals or passersby. Just as he tenses up and is about to go into a bark frenzy, push the button on the reinforcement level, say *leave it*, and then call your dog to you. Then reward him for coming when called. You will have to be persistent because a certain amount of territoriality is natural for dogs. A few barks are not uncalled for, but he should cease and desist when you say *leave it*. For more information, see "Nuisance barking/whining." For barking in the car, have a passenger along to hold the e-collar remote control. Anticipate his barking at the reinforcement level when you see him thinking about it. Say *leave it*.

Barks at television. Same as "Barks at animals or people out of the windows."

Play biting. Sleep deprivation is the most common cause of excessive play biting in dogs under 1 year of age, especially dogs who live with young children. Before trying any form of correction, put your dog on a crate napping schedule of 1-hour nap time followed by an hour of playtime, and continue to rotate on this schedule for at least 4 days to see if play biting diminishes. Also note if certain actions on your part precipitate the biting, such as overexcitement that you may unintentionally cause. If all else fails, put your dog on a leash, and when he play bites, say *leave it* as you push the constant button set at the education level. Then give him a command which you can calmly reward, such as sit. It may help to redirect his attention to a bone or toy he is allowed to chew.

Jumps on people at the door or elsewhere. Be prepared for situations where your dog is likely to jump on you or guests. For the first week, try to have your dog on leash, training collar, and e-collar. Ask your guests to ignore the dog. Say *leave it* and push the constant button on the educational level for jumping, then ask him to sit. You or your guest can quietly pet the dog while he is sitting. You may use vibration for jumping, but only if it does not scare your dog. It's a good thing that he is happy to see people. We want to correct jumping but not harshly.

Excessive licking of people, objects, or self. It is important to rule out medical reasons if your dog obsessively licks himself in a specific place, such as his paws. Allergies, injury, arthritis, or infection are common reasons why dogs lick themselves to the point where they may lose hair. Assuming your veterinarian determines no medical causation, you may wish to use an unpleasant-tasting chew deterrent spray to decrease licking. Your veterinarian or pet store can recommend one. You can also use the e-collar to lightly distract your dog from what could simply have turned into a nervous habit, but be sure you are providing adequate exercise and mental stimulation. Say *leave it* as you push the button, which should be set quite low. Start a little below your normal educational level because chances are your dog will be relatively calm at this moment. Provide a chew toy for your dog to refocus him on something more productive. The same process holds true if he is excessively licking you. Interrupt the behavior as described, but do not exceed the educational level. We do not wish the dog to be penalized for being near you.

Plays keep-away with stolen objects. Be observant so you can catch your dog just as he is about to grab a sock from the laundry basket or any other forbidden item he often takes. Just as he makes contact with the item, push the button on the reinforcement level, say *leave it*, and then call your dog to you. If he brings the item to you when he comes, gently remove it from his mouth. If he will not release the item, push the vibration button, say *leave it*, and take the item. Then reward your dog for coming when called.

Chases cat. We place this in the Spoken Leave It section rather than the silent version because we want your dog to learn that you object to his unduly bothering the cat. You'll need to observe all dog/cat interactions for 1 month so your dog cannot successfully chase the cat when unobserved. Place your dog on the long line attached to his training collar. You don't need to hold the line, but you'll step on it if he does not respond when you say *leave it* and push the button on the reinforcement level. Do that at the first sign your dog fixates on the cat and is about to give chase. Never leave your dog unattended wearing his training lines or equipment. And if you believe your dog would harm your cat, use extreme caution. Do not leave them alone together.

Chasing cars, bikes, skateboards. Place a training collar with 6-foot leash attached and an e-collar on the dog. As you encounter these triggers on your daily walks, treat them as you would any other distraction your dog inappropriately reacts to. In the instant before they go into prey or defensive drive and lunge, most dogs will fixate on the distraction for a fraction of a second. In that instant, say *leave it* and push the button using the reinforcement level. Simultaneously make an abrupt turn away from the distraction and continue to walk briskly. Because prey drive puts dogs into a high excitement state of mind, you may have to experiment with an interrupter level until you find the one that adequately gets his attention. Start at the educational level, and use that for a few days. But don't be surprised if eventually you must go to reinforcement level or a bit higher than normal. Be sure to lower your level again once the distraction has passed. If possible, begin practicing far from the distraction and work your way closer over time. In the case of car chasing, eventually you should be able to use the recall to stop an off-leash dog before he chases. See Lessons 8, 10, and 11.

Bolts from crate. Review Lesson 3. You may wish to practice unloading your dog from the crate while he is wearing an e-collar. Approach the crate without speaking, and if he begins to thrash about, walk away. Continue until your dog allows you to approach without fussing. When you are at the door but not touching it, ask your dog to sit. You may tap the momentary button if necessary.

Then crack the door, reach in, and connect your leash *while the dog is still in the crate*. Lead him out of the crate calmly. Repeat this for a week.

Bolts from car. Slightly open the car door and use your body to block the opening. Then use the same solution as above for the crate.

Jumps from back seat of car into front seat. If you plan to work on this while the car is moving, *don't drive*. Put your arm and elbow into the gap through which the dog jumps from back to front. Tap or briefly hold the constant button on the reinforcement level, saying *leave it* when your dog makes physical contact with your arm. When he stops trying to come forward, praise very quietly. If you have an excitable dog likely to overreact to praise, say nothing. For safety, some people use a special harness to buckle their dogs into the back seat. Most dogs quickly become used to these harnesses.

Some Behavioral Problems Are Caused by Anxiety

The connection between anxiety and behavior issues is real. That being said, failure to provide adequate exercise, human contact, rules, and mental stimulation can cause anxiety in dogs, which can best be alleviated by supplying those missing elements. When used artfully with our method, the e-collar is a good tool for training dogs so they may enjoy more liberty and freedom from conflict. However, we do not view it as a cure-all. Consider whether you need to increase the quality of critical areas of your dog's life before applying the solutions below. If you need help fulfilling your dog's needs, remember you have options such as dog daycare, a dog walker, a pet sitter, or a friendly neighbor. Even more information and assistance for canine anxiety can be found in our book, *Let Dogs Be Dogs*. And it's never wrong to consult your veterinarian.

Light or shadow chasing, spinning or tail chasing, or staring. This is an obsessive-compulsive behavior that sounds or looks amusing at first, but it can become debilitating to dogs. Prevention is the best approach. Never play "chase the light" with a laser pointer or flashlight. Unlike cats, many dogs become fixated on it to the point where any glare from a window pane causes them to stare obsessively, even for hours on end. If your dog already has this problem, use the e-collar to gently interrupt it by calling the dog to you or by sending the dog to his bed, then rewarding on the bed. We find that if you consistently interrupt this behavior with gently reinforced commands that snap them out of it, many dogs will stop doing the behavior or sharply reduce the intensity of it. In extreme cases, ask your veterinarian about medical assistance.

Problems Caused by Aggression Have a Number of Solutions

What people label as "aggression" can range from barking through a window at passersby all the way up through biting family members or fighting other dogs. The former is less serious than the latter and can usually be reduced by good training from an owner whom the dog respects.

WARNING: For any serious aggression issue, or if your dog has a bite history, please consult a professional dog trainer instead of following our training program. We define a dog with serious aggression as one that has bitten a person or pet, or one you believe may eventually do so. In such cases, it is best to err on the side of caution and seek professional help.

Aggressive to smaller dogs on the walk. See "Chasing cars, bikes, skateboards" in Lesson 16.

Barks or lunges at people, dogs, squirrels, or animals on the walk. This is often called leash aggression. Treat the same as "Chasing cars, bikes, skateboards" in Lesson 16.

Aggressive to invited guests in the home, hallway, elevator, or lobby. In the home, use the *place* command to prevent your dog from challenging guests. Do not permit your dog to approach invited guests in a challenging manner. Have your dog on a leash, training collar, and e-collar. If necessary, say *leave it* as you use the educational level to direct your dog to his bed. If your dog relaxes and seems ready to be polite to your guest, let him off the bed, hold the leash, and allow him to greet the visitor. If you live in a building and your dog is aggressive in the hall or lobby, treat the same as "Chasing cars, bikes, skateboards." Aggression toward people or dogs in the elevator is much more difficult because of the confined space. Use and reinforce the *sit* command. You may also find it beneficial to use an additional piece of equipment such as a basket muzzle or a calming cap, which is a sort of blindfold that serves to reduce but not completely eliminate the dog's visual field. If you need either of those, introduce them slowly over the course of a week before using them in the elevator. If your dog has bitten a person or if you are concerned that he will bite someone, please contact a professional dog trainer for assistance.

Overprotective. We define overprotective as a dog's tendency to bark or growl inappropriately when nonthreatening people or other dogs approach you. In the home, use the *go to place* command to show your dog you want him to move out of your personal space. This often helps the dog understand he is not permitted to be overprotective of you. Should he exhibit this behavior outside of the home on the Purposeful Walk, tap the constant button on the educational level and turn. Then turn back and continue on your way. Repeat if needed. Over time you may need to increase to your reinforcement level.

Aggressive to invited guests in the yard. If your dog objects to guests moving around your yard, put him on a leash for optimal control. If you trust that he will not bite your guest, you can put him on a long line and e-collar. Use the Spoken Leave It, combined with the educational level if needed, and then immediately use the *come* command to call your dog. *If you train your dog with the entire lesson plan in this book*, most dogs will stop low-level aggressive behavior when you curtail their freedom of movement and give commands that interrupt the behavior and show them you do not approve.

Aggressive to *uninvited or unexpected* guests in the home or yard.
We sometimes hear from owners who are surprised that their dog acted

aggressively to someone who entered the yard or home uninvited or unexpectedly. Remember that meter readers might enter your yard. Neighborhood children might climb your fence to retrieve a lost ball. Imagine a friend calls from the driveway. You know them well but your dog knows them only casually or not at all. You answer the phone from upstairs and tell them to come in. Your dog may be unable to distinguish an innocent incursion from one which is not innocent, and he may act aggressively. The only solution, particularly if your dog is not overtly friendly to everyone regardless of circumstance, is to personally greet people at the door rather than allow them to admit themselves into your home. Don't send young children to let people in, and understand you're taking a chance if you leave your dog alone in the yard, even if you have a fence with locked gates.

Barks at people or dogs when in the car. Don't drive if you plan to work on this behavior while the car is moving. Park at a distance from what will cause your dog to bark. Remain in the vehicle. When your dog becomes reactive, tap the constant button on the reinforcement level as you say *leave it*. Praise calmly when your dog quiets, even for a moment. Repeat as needed but practice first at a distance. Over the course of 1 week, move closer until, for example, you can go through a drive-through without a big reaction from your dog.

Resource Guarding Can Start Out Looking Cute, But It Can Get Ugly Fast

Some people accidentally teach their dogs to guard resources by playfully snatching away toys or by being overinvolved with their dog's food. And some people have done everything right but find they own unreasonably possessive dogs. If you have serious problems with resource guarding, we believe you will find food for thought in the solutions below. Consult *Let Dogs Be Dogs* for a great deal more information about how to deal with resources in a healthy way to prevent resource guarding. And as with any problem involving aggression or actual bites, please consult an experienced professional dog trainer, especially if you have children. The solutions below are not comprehensive for every possible situation, but they will give you ideas and alternatives.

Guards food. Avoid being *overinvolved* with your dog's food. Some people insist their dog eat while their hand is in the bowl, or they constantly take away the food as matter of routine. If you're concerned about your dog's attitude toward food, a better idea is to occasionally feed your dog his meal, one handful at a time, in return for performing an obedience command you have taught him. Call him to come and sit. Then you can put a handful of his food in his bowl and allow him to eat it. Ask for a 3-minute down. Then feed more. If you're not squeamish about the idea, there is also some benefit from feeding that handful right out of your hand. Punishment for guarding food is rarely, if ever, advisable. Instead, show your dog that you will be involved with his food, but that you are a fair and predictable *provider* of that food, rather than an unfair, unpredictable *taker*. Use the e-collar to reinforce commands as necessary. Do not try to punish food guarding directly with an e-collar.

Guards space. If your dog growls when you or anyone else sits near him on furniture or in your bed, you should strongly consider switching to a "no furniture" and "no human bed" policy. If your dog has bitten under these conditions, you should absolutely make and enforce those changes. Use the *go to place* command so your dog can be comfortable in his own space. If your dog is just starting to lightly guard space, you may be able to fix the situation. Leave his long line attached only when you're observing, and at the first sign of guarding, stand up, push the button on the educational level, and if necessary use the line to guide him to a nearby dog bed. See "Jumps on furniture he shouldn't." Also see Lesson 14, Go to Place.

Guards toys. First let's define terms. Your dog views rawhide, bully sticks, antlers, and chew hooves as food, not toys. If your dog is very possessive of those, consider eliminating them, especially if your dog is aggressive to people or other dogs when guarding them. Alternatively, you can give them to your dog only in his crate, which will make his time there more pleasant. However, if he growls at you when guarding his dog toys, then use the Spoken Leave It so he will either drop or give you the toy. When he does that, call him to you and give a treat so he learns that you take but that you also give and reward. Consider putting his toys away and occasionally offering your dog a toy in return for a sit or other obedience command.

Guards the human. Some clients report the dog will growl at or even bite anyone who gets too close to them when he is sitting in their lap or lying next to them on the sofa or bed. For 1 month, eliminate lap, furniture, and bed time. Instead use the *go to place* command—and an e-collar set to educational level if necessary—to send your dog to his place when you want other people to sit close to you or when you want children on your lap. If the issue is relatively low level, you'll likely be able to restore furniture or bed privileges. But if this is a serious problem, strongly consider switching to a permanent "no furniture" and "no human bed" policy. See "Jumps on furniture he shouldn't." Also see Lesson 14, Go to Place.

Problems Involving More Than One Dog

Dogs are social pack animals and are naturally drawn together, yet many dogs are not well socialized in the critical weeks and months of their puppyhood. This can cause problems, especially if you have more than one dog in the home. As a general principle, you as Pack Leader should be looking to reduce or eliminate any need your dogs may feel to compete for resources. Competition among dogs who live in the same home usually means that the owner is not taking a sufficiently active role as Pack Leader. This can lead to disharmony and, in some cases, dog fights. Individually train all dogs living in your household for best results. Many e-collar manufacturers offer collar systems which are expandable to accommodate more than one dog. This can be very handy indeed. But remember, for each dog to understand the collar, you must train them.

Plays too roughly with other dogs. Certain dogs are highly social but have a play style that overwhelms other dogs. At the first sign your dog is playfully biting at the neck of another dog or otherwise playing too rough, use the Spoken Leave It and push either the constant button set to the educational level or the vibration button. Repeat as needed. This will show your dog he is allowed to play but that he is not to exceed the limits you set.

If your dog is humping or playing too hard with another dog at the dog park, you also can apply this solution. Remember to tell him leave it so he knows the correction is coming from you and not the other dog. If you want to interrupt a situation in which both dogs are playing too hard, don't use the e-collar. Instead, use unaggressive physical intervention so you can stop both dogs at the same time. If necessary, separate the dogs.

Won't come when playing with other dogs or in dog park. You may need to revisit and practice the *come* command as applied in Lessons 8 through 13. When playing with other dogs, coming to you is one of the most difficult tasks you can ask of your dog. But it is important. After reviewing the lessons, call your dog as you tap the constant button on reinforcement level. Chances are he won't feel it any lower than that because play is so distracting. A word of warning, though: Call your dog when he can disengage from the other dog or dogs. It's not the right time if he's on the bottom of a dog pile.

Older dog is aggressive to puppy. Most older dogs enjoy puppies, but very often a puppy will rudely push right into the face of the older dog. Sometimes puppies relentlessly pounce on older dogs who find the rough play painful because they have a touch of arthritis. You can prevent and sometimes even fix this problem by advocating for your older dog. Attach a long line to the puppy's collar (only when you're closely observing, as with all equipment), and simply don't allow the puppy to overwhelm your older dog. If your older dog is unfairly domineering a puppy who is behaving well in his presence, use the Spoken Leave It as needed. Teach your puppy how to be polite to your older dog, and teach the older dog that the puppy falls under your protection. Ideally, and in most cases, a loving relationship will develop.

FREQUENTLY ASKED QUESTIONS

How old should my dog be before I start e-collar training?

At least age 5 months. See the Introduction (page 9) for more advice about working with a puppy.

What should I do if I need more help than I find in the book?

Since the initial publication of *The Art of Training Your Dog*, we have created a Facebook group, The Art of Training Your Dog with an Ecollar, which has helped thousands of dog owners. This collection of frequently asked questions is inspired by certain questions have arisen repeatedly on that forum. You can learn more about this book and that group at TheArtOfTrainingYourDog.com.

My dog had previous training with a different method. If he knows some of the commands already, can I save time by skipping certain steps or lessons?

No, start from the beginning, with Lesson 1. Our method is sequential. Each lesson builds on elements of the previous lesson. If you skip steps, even the first one, you may skip the reliability and results you want. Use the Lesson Planner (page 253) to stay on schedule.

What can I do to make it easier for my dog to learn the training?

Here's a simple trick. We highly recommend crating your dog for 20 minutes before and after each training session.

Crating before the lesson gives her a moment to relax; plus, she'll be grateful for the attention when you begin to train. When it's time to let her out of the crate to train, first connect the training collar to the leash. Then open the door only slightly as you simultaneously put the training collar on your dog. This order of operations gives you control from the moment you're ready to train. It also teaches your dog to come out of the crate calmly rather than jumping and overexcited.

Crating 20 minutes after the lesson allows your dog time to relax and process what she just learned. Just as Italian food tastes better the second day, your dog also needs time to marinate on the new ideas and skills that you just taught her.

Can more than one family member do training lessons with our dog?

Yes, but we advise that only adults do the training. A child shouldn't handle an e-collar or take a dog off the property without an adult present. But more than one family member can practice with the dog as long as each person has read the book and knows what lessons and levels the others have practiced. Keep notes for one another in the Lesson Planner (page 253). It's important to take the dog through each lesson in order and for the recommended number of repetitions and days. Constantly swapping handlers may slow the dog's progress. Another option is for one person to take the dog all the way through the program and for a second person to begin with Lesson 4.

Can I let my dog play wild games every day for exercise in the months I'm doing the training?

This is a judgment call on your part. All good games have rules. If your dog will play politely, have at it by all means. But if he can't play without jumping on you or plays keep away with laundry and so forth, you're better off suspending wild play until you've completed training. That's when you'll have better control over the game and can prevent it from undoing the good behavior you're teaching. Remember: *Training is draining*. If your dog seems bored and has excess energy, add an additional session or two to your day. Your dog will learn more as you help him burn that extra energy.

Does my dog need her usual walks for exercise even though we're not up to Lesson 6 and the outdoor Purposeful Walk?

This is another judgment call. If your dog behaves reasonably on walks, then you can continue, and they'll improve once you begin Lesson 6. If your walks feel like a disaster, wait until you're doing Lesson 6, which then becomes the norm for good, daily walks. In the meantime, training is draining, so add an additional daily training session if your dog is getting antsy before Lesson 6.

I have two dogs. Can I walk them together?

Eventually, yes, but teach each dog individually through full competence in Lesson 6. When each behaves well during the Lesson 6 Purposeful Walks, you can begin to walk them together, ideally with a different person handling each dog. Eventually you can try walking them together, either one leash in each hand or both dogs on one side with both leashes in that hand. Some people with similar sized dogs use a coupler with snaps on each end to connect one dog's collar to the other. A single leash then snaps in the middle of the coupler so you can walk two dogs with one leash. This variation requires both dogs to be well trained individually and very familiar with Lesson 6, but many people can make it work afterward. Of course, the benefit is that you all can exercise together, which saves time.

If a loose dog approaches when I'm doing the outdoor lessons or walking my dog, what should I do?

Loose dogs can pose a problem because you're controlling yours but no one's controlling the other dog. You can't always know what it will do. Ideally you just experience a brief, annoying encounter, and if you ask, an apologetic owner will come secure his dog. But sometimes an oncoming dog may have aggressive intentions. A few products can repel a loose, aggressive dog if necessary. These include spray cans that emit a stream of a harmless repellant. If you're concerned, you can purchase one of them, but ensure that the product meets local regulations.

To be clear, we don't advocate taking action against a loose dog who simply may be impolite or trying to play with yours. In case of extreme aggression, a quick spray of harmless repellant is certainly better than serious injury to you or the dogs. If you live in a neighborhood where this problem is constant, consider driving your dog to a calmer area for the outdoor training lessons or Purposeful Walks.

My dog is used to a choke chain, harness, or head halter. Can I use it during the training?

We highly recommend that you stick to the equipment recommended in Chapter 5. It may not be apparent at first, but as the lessons progress, you'll find significant disadvantages to training collars not listed in the chapter.

When it's time to use the e-collar, can I use vibration for everything?

You might think that your dog will prefer vibration, but few dogs do. When they feel vibration, many startle. Others don't care at all. But we don't want either of those reactions. Most dogs react much better to a brief, low-level tap of electronic stimulation from a good e-collar reviewed in Chapter 5. We also find that, if vibration is used as more than an occasional reminder, many dogs learn to tune it out. Electronic stimulation is variable and unique, so it catches the dog's attention without startling. See Chapter 6 for more details.

What can I use the tone button for?

Some e-collars have a tone button, but we don't find it useful for our method or an important feature. We're training for eventual high-distraction activities and environments. It's very unlikely that, when chasing a rabbit into the road, your dog will respond to, let alone hear, a tone.

My dog has annoying problem behaviors. Can I do something about those right away?

You might need to make more liberal use of the crate temporarily or observe more carefully so you can interrupt problem behaviors. Once you've gone through the training program—only 6 weeks—you can apply the solutions in the Appendix of Dog Behavior Problems (page 257). If you skip the training process, you might not have an easy time applying the solutions. Be patient and review the Appendix. You'll find about 50 problem behaviors and solutions there.

I have an electronic fence, and my dog is trained to it already. Is there anything special I need to know about training with an e-collar?

Don't train with the e-collar in any area with an e-fence until your dog has become very familiar with e-collar training. A good rule of thumb: Avoid training in an e-fence area until your dog has become comfortable with Lesson 12 in other locations. If you begin training behind the fence before that point, your dog may worry that you moved the fence, even though the e-collar level is much lower than the e-fence level.

Can my dog wear the e-fence collar and the e-collar at the same time?

Yes, for the brief amount of time that you'd need both on your dog.

Can I use the e-collar for boundary training so my dog will stay in the yard even when I'm not there?

No, we don't recommend this. Dog training works best when you're present to communicate with your dog, especially in case of distractions such as rabbits or squirrels.

Lesson 1 seems so basic. Can I just skip it?

No, don't skip Lesson 1. This lesson teaches your dog two critical skills. When you hold the leash close to you, without putting tension on the dog, your dog learns that he shouldn't leave nor pester you or anyone else. That's exactly what you need from him during any number of real-life activities such as signing in at the vet or stopping to talk to a neighbor.

An added benefit of Lesson 1 as written in the Lesson Plan is that, once he has gotten good at it, you can apply the same principles when you sit down. Your dog will learn to relax calmly near you without straining on the leash or pestering. Again, this is what you'll need if sitting in an office with your dog or other similar situations. First teach the lesson while standing, as shown in the pictures. Eventually, you can work on it at convenient times in your day, when sitting. When you begin, your dog likely will try jumping in your lap. Rather than pushing him off, a game which delights the average dog, try stepping on the leash so that your dog feels no tension when not jumping but self-corrects when he jumps.

In Lesson 1, my dog whines and will not relax. What do I do?

Lesson 1 lasts only 5 minutes, but that may not be enough time for a very whiny dog to relax or quiet himself for a moment. We recommend that you practice the lesson in a calm environment with few distractions. If you have another pet, for example, remove it from the area for the few moments that Lesson 1 requires. Do the lesson as described, but try not to end when your dog is mid-whine. A point will come when the dog stops whining, even for an instant, to look up at you in confusion, and that's the perfect moment to end the lesson quietly.

In Lesson 2, my dog lags behind me. What should I do?

If your dog usually pulls, you might find it startling for your dog to walk slightly behind rather than lunging ahead of you. In this case, it's not a problem. She probably is trying to figure out what you want. You'll make it easier on her by maintaining your purposeful pace. On the other hand, if your dog is lagging more than a foot behind you or stopping hard, see the lesson description for suggestions. Some dogs aren't protesting so much as expressing confusion, especially if being trained in small spaces. An apartment dweller with a lagging dog may find it useful to shift Lesson 2 to a longer hallway outside the front door. A homeowner can try training on a back patio, for example. In any case, don't worry about it too much. Lesson 2 concludes after only 3 days of practice. When you started training, you probably wished that your dog would slow down anyway!

In Lesson 2, even after a couple of sessions, my dog is pulling hard. What should I do?

Create a low-distraction environment when you begin the lesson. If that doesn't help, you likely will find it beneficial to change to a slightly more corrective training collar. See Chapter 5 for details. For example, if you're training on a Starmark collar, switching to a prong collar might make a world of difference.

In Lesson 4, my dog won't stay by me. She doesn't pull, but she doesn't want to go or lags behind, which didn't happen in Lesson 2. What do I do?

Try lowering the e-collar level to see if perhaps it was set too high for her comfort, or try moving the lesson outdoors to a low-distraction environment, such as a deck or patio. If you live in an apartment or condo, you can train in a long corridor outside your door. Remember, you'll be past this lesson in a few days, and you'll be walking outdoors, which is more interesting for your dog.

In Lesson 4, after I stop for sit or a brief rest, my dog jumps on me when I look at her. What should I do?

At such moments, try not to make eye contact with your dog. Use only brief peripheral vision to check what she's doing, then resume the lesson. If that doesn't work, resume the instant your dog begins to jump. She'll learn quickly that jumping will be interrupted rather than discussed.

Lessons 2 and 4 went fine, but now that we're doing Lesson 6, my dog is pulling hard, especially with major distractions. What do I do?
Try teaching the lesson right in front of your house or in a less distracting area. For the first few days, you don't need to go all the way around the block or neighborhood. Prioritize good behavior for the allotted time rather than the distance travelled. If that doesn't help, you may find it beneficial to change to a more corrective collar. See Chapter 5 for details. For example, if training on a Starmark collar, try a prong collar instead. A training collar that worked fine in the house might not prove as effective when you're outside amid real-world distractions. Selecting the correct equipment usually yields far better results.

In Lesson 6, my dog isn't pulling or putting much tension on the leash, but he's getting ahead of me or trying to switch sides. What should I do?
Shorten the leash a little, not enough to tighten the training collar but enough so that he can't get much ahead of you or switch sides without tightening it himself. If necessary, use your leash hand to guide him quickly back to where you want him to be, which is also where the training collar will feel loose.

ACKNOWLEDGMENTS

The friendship between the authors started quite by accident. In one another, we found like minds, whose differences create strengths rather than weaknesses. We are indebted to each other and, indeed, to the entire New Skete community.

Although is customary to thank one's literary agent, Kate Hartson dedicated herself to the formation, writing, and photographing of this book in ways that we do not believe are at all customary. She found our dynamic new publisher, helped us find our voice, opened her home to us, and then literally went on the road to support us as we did the photography. Kate, thank you for your friendship and for taking this book from dream to reality. Vincent Remini, our long-suffering photographer, chauffer, fixer, political pundit, and food critic, took literally thousands of pictures under often frustrating conditions. We are deeply grateful.

We hoped for the understanding and guidance of our editor, Ann Treistman, as we wrote this book. What we could not have expected was for Ann to come to the monastery for 5 days with her dog, Molly, to train alongside the other students at one of the e-collar workshops that the authors teach (see page 246). Not only was this above and beyond the call of duty, but also we believe that week brought this book to life for Ann before it was ever written. Since then she has provided invaluable assistance in its creation and we are very grateful for this relationship.

Many people have influenced and assisted us over the years. Although this list is incomplete, we would like to thank them for the support and friendship. Mary Mazzeri, for decades of generosity. Martin Deeley, gone too soon. Patrick Farrell, for always believing. Aaron Pfeiffer, always our cheerleader. The New Skete community, Ida Williams, Jack and Wendy Volhard, Colleen Goldberg, Samantha Mason, Faye Meade, William Goldberg, the Pensacks, Florence Dear, Clyde Anderson, and many friends inside and outside of the International Association of Canine Professionals dog training community.

INDEX

ABOUT THE AUTHORS

The Monks of New Skete have been breeding and raising German shepherds, as well as training dogs of all breeds for more than 40 years. They are the authors of *The Art of Raising a Puppy, How to Be Your Dog's Best Friend*, and more. Their books have sold a combined total of over 1 million copies. The monks note, "For many of us, love for creation deepens through the relationships we form with our pets, particularly our dogs."

The monks' relationship with dogs began in the early days of the monastery when they were given a German shepherd named Kyr. He quickly became a beloved pet who led the monks to adopt more German shepherds. Eventually, at the request of friends, they began breeding these beautiful and intelligent animals. They wrote their first bestseller at the request of a dog training client who was also a book editor. No one was more surprised at their eventual celebrity than the monks. The New Skete Monastery is located in Cambridge, New York. Visit the monks at newskete.org.

Marc Goldberg has been training dogs since he was a child. Winning multiple AKC obedience competitions early on gave him a quick start, but he was eventually to find more satisfaction in helping others enjoy their dogs than in winning trophies. Now Marc is a nationally renowned dog trainer and former president of the International Association of Canine Professionals. He introduced e-collar training to the Monks of New Skete, and he is the coauthor, with the monks, of *Let Dogs Be Dogs*. Marc is based near Chicago, Illinois, training for clients at his Little Dog Farm. He lives with his partner and their three beloved dogs: Scooter, a rat terrier; Tippy, a border collie mix; and Friday, a German shepherd. Visit Marc at chicagodogtrainer.com.

Together, the authors teach seminars featuring their dog training method. The seminars are popular with dog owners and trainers alike. Learn more at theartoftrainingyourdog.com.